AUERBACH ON MINICOMPUTERS

AUERBACH ON series

Published:

Optical Character Recognition
Alphanumeric Displays
Automatic Photocomposition
Microfilm Readers/Printers
Digital Plotters and Image Digitizers
Computer Output Microfilm
Data Collection Systems
Time Sharing
Small Business Computers
Minicomputers

Coming:

Data Communications Terminals
Data Entry Systems
Systems Software
Large Scale Memories
Data Communications
Software for Business Accounting

AUERBACH ON

MINICOMPUTERS

First Edition

petrocelli books, New York 1974

First Printing

Printed in the United States of America

Library of Congress Cataloging in Publication Data

Petrocelli Books.
   Auerbach on minicomputers.

   "An expansion of material derived from Auerbach
minicomputer reports (AMCR) and the Auerbach technology
evaluation service minicomputer study."
   1. Miniature computers. I. Auerbach Publishers.
II. Title.
TK7888.3.P46 1974   621.3819'5   73-17204
ISBN 0-88405-024-6

CONTENTS

PREFACE

This volume is one of a series of books covering significant developments in the information science industry. *AUERBACH On Minicomputers* deals with small, stored-program computers costing under $25,000. Minicomputers have evolved as the need for small processors became apparent and as technological developments provided cost and size reductions. Due to their flexibility, minicomputers are used in a variety of industries and applications. They function as controllers for processes, devices, and communication systems, and fill a basic need for low-cost computation.

The minicomputer industry has experienced rapid growth in the past several years. This growth has been accomplished despite the depressed state of the general economy and the sluggishness in the total computer industry.

The relatively low price of minicomputers as compared to that of larger general-purpose computers is achieved by shorter word lengths, simpler instruction sets, smaller memories, less elaborate input/output capabilities, smaller peripheral devices, less software, and less market support. Due principally to progress in semiconductor technology, minicomputer prices have declined an average of 18 percent per year since the mid-1960s. Further progress in semiconductor technology should produce additional price declines. With continuing price declines and reductions in the number of separate packages in the central processor, minicomputers are rapidly approaching the status of a component of larger systems.

Because of the low cost and great flexibility of minicomputers, the potential market for these machines is enormous. As prices for minicomputer central processors continue to decline, this market broadens to include all activities associated with industrial and consumer products. The primary limiting factor of wider minicomputer use is the inability of industry and commerce to identify and implement new applications. This is, of course, difficult for the less sophisticated users unless the marketing approach offers assistance and direction.

Successful penetration of potential markets and continued growth of the industry will also depend on the manufacturers' ability to simplify the application of minicomputers by providing greater support in software packages, education, and training. Another inducement would be the design of flexible systems that would use nearly identical hardware and software adaptable to various applications within a user's area of interest.

The number of minicomputer manufacturers grew rapidly in the late 1960s and comprised not only the older, more diversified companies but also those newly formed and dedicated to minicomputers. Although continued growth of the market and constant improvement of the machines indicated wide opportunity for all these companies, technological change and a reorientation of marketing requirements has resulted in a more sophisticated structuring of the industry in the early 1970s. Thus, the ultimate success of minicomputer manufacturers will be determined by their ability to provide additional products and services such as computer peripherals, software, and completely packaged systems that can satisfy user needs.

AUERBACH on Minicomputers is an expansion of material derived from *AUERBACH Minicomputer Reports* (AMCR) and *The AUERBACH Technology Evaluation Service* Minicomputer Study. AMCR is a major unit in the *AUERBACH Computer Technology Reports,* a looseleaf reference service recognized as the standard guide to EDP throughout the world. It is prepared and edited by the publisher's staff of professional EDP specialists.

The material in this volume was prepared by the staff of AUERBACH Publishers Inc., and has been updated prior to publication. Due to the rapid changes occurring in the field, however, the currentness and completeness of the contents cannot be guaranteed.

1. THE MINICOMPUTER IN PERSPECTIVE

Few developments of recent times have so captured the public's imagination as the advent of the computer. Fueled at first by the fanciful predictions of the press, the public's flights of fancy acquired a momentum of their own, and through an imaginative, if untutored, blending of the concepts of robotics and mathematics, created a host of remarkable expectations.

Surprisingly, the speculations and prophecies of 20 years ago, which then seemed so extravagant, have in many cases been realized and even far surpassed. As predicted, computers exert impact on our daily lives. They run our industries, manage our money, control our communications, direct our traffic, assist in educating our children, and guide our probings into space. But more surprising, in many cases the computers are not the "giant brains" of the early predictions, but are small units scarcely larger than a desk drawer. These "mini" computers (see Fig. 1-1) are smaller by a factor of 1000 or more to 1, in comparison to their huge predecessors of 20 years ago, but they are more powerful and cost less than one hundredth as much. Their low price and their processing power make them cost effective in a remarkable variety of applications. Minicomputers embody the revolutionary advances in semiconductor technology of the past decade, and may one day be as commonplace and necessary as a family's second car.

THE MINICOMPUTER DEFINED

The word "minicomputer" probably originated in a paper presented at the Fall Joint Computer Conference in 1968,[1] which described a small ex-

[1]D.C. Hitt, G.H. Ottaway, and R.W. Shirk, "The Mini-Computer—A New Approach to Computer Design," Conference Proceedings, Vol. 33, Part 1, 1968.

FIG. 1-1.   Digital Computer Corporation (DEC) PDP-11.

perimental computer designed by IBM. This model contained only 8 program instructions and 512 bytes of memory, and was appropriately called "MINI ." During 1969 the word "minicomputer" gained currency as a generic descriptor of the many small computers that were introduced to satisfy the demands of the scientific, data communications, and control-computer markets for a low-cost machine.

Minicomputers cannot be defined rigidly, since the dynamic nature of the industry precludes static design. Any definition must be flexible, changing as the minicomputer industry responds to technological and market opportunities in innovative ways. The description given below, however, characterizes a distinguishable segment of the data processing industry and corresponds to general industry usage. A minicomputer is a small, stored-program digital computer that can be programmed in an assembly or higher-level language and which has the following attributes:

1. Sells for less than $25,000 for a minimum, stand-alone configuration comprised of a central processing unit, memory, input/output equipment, and system software.

2. Contains a memory of at least 4000 eight-bit words.

3. Performs normal computer functions (inputs, transfers, stores, processes, and outputs data) under stored-program control.

4. Is usable in a broad range of applications.

This book will deal with computers bounded by these specific characteristics.

Comparison between Minicomputers and Larger Machines

Minicomputers are functionally similar to their larger counterparts. The implications of the description "mini" should not be misconstrued. These are powerful machines, with speeds as fast as or even faster than larger computers. Their low cost in comparison to that of large computers results from the following characteristics:

1. All have simple instruction sets, both in absolute number and the power of instructions provided.

2. All have small memories. System prices under $5000 are for minimum configurations, typically with 4000-word memory. For larger systems, memory prices alone rapidly exceed the central processor cost.

3. Word length is short, which permits design economies in the central processor electronics.

4. All have simple input/output (I/O) control capabilities.

5. Elimination of such features as real-time clocks and parity checking from the basic system is cost inhibitive.

6. Slow and relatively unsophisticated peripheral devices are used.

7. Minimal system engineering support is needed.

8. A limited amount of comprehensive system software is supplied free with a system.

Although minicomputers can be distinguished from larger general-purpose computers, the distinctions are becoming less clear as general-purpose computers decline in price and become more modular. Also, some general-purpose systems are composed of multiple processors, one of which may be a small computer. The capability of minicomputers, on the other hand, is increased by the addition of more memory, peripherals, and software, so that some configurations offer almost all the capabilities of larger systems. Thus, the low end of a general-purpose computer line tends to overlap the high end of a minicomputer line.

System Overview

Minicomputer designs emphasize flexibility to satisfy a broad range of application requirements. They are typically designed around a minimum stand-alone system composed of a central processor, a small core memory of 4000 words, and a Teletype keyboard/printer with paper tape input/output. This basic system can operate as a stand-alone computer; it usually includes a minimum of standard hardware, but it can accommodate a variety of optional hardware modules to produce a system matched to a user's specific requirements.

Systems are usually also available for the OEM (Original Equipment Manufacture) market (Fig. 1-2), where the buyer configures a system from the OEM "shopping list," develops software for a specific application, and sells the whole package to the end user. These are usually turnkey systems; that is, the middle man does all the work associated with the installation and all the user has to do is "turn the key."

The systems offered to the OEM (original equipment manufacturer) market are stripped basic systems with simple cabinetry and control panels, sometimes with no cabinetry at all, and only rack-mountable components

Figure 1-2.   Computer Automation, Inc. OEM computer line—ALPHA (left front), Jumbo ALPHA (left rear), NAKED MINI (right front), Jumbo NAKED MINI (right rear).

These systems are so modular that the list of components available with or without prices has come to be called a "shopping list."

Although the OEM market is an important part of the minicomputer industry and will often be mentioned, the minicomputers described in this book will be end-user systems. These are systems the manufacturers develop and sell or lease to the end-user.

Minicomputer options include: memory parity checking, memory protection, additional memory, priority interrupt system, and additional input/output (I/O) channels. A full range of peripheral devices are also available: card readers/punches, disks, tapes, line printers, serial printers, plotters, CRT terminals, data communications interfaces and multiplexers, and analog/digital or digital/analog conversation equipment. Minicomputers are not so "mini" when a considerable number of optional features are included.

All minicomputers are binary machines, that is, they use two-value logic: yes or no, 1 or zero, true or false. All perform binary arithmetic. Subroutines must be used to convert data from decimal to binary on input and from binary to decimal on output.

Word length, the amount of data that can be stored in one memory location, ranges from 8 to 24 bits, the equivalent of 2.25 to 7.16 decimal digits. By far the most popular word length is 16 bits, equivalent ot 4.6 decimal digits. It is so popular it is almost an industry standard. The popularity of DEC's (Digital Equipment Corporation) PDP-8, which uses a 12-bit word, and PDP-15, which uses an 18-bit word, persists, however.

The 16-bit word has many advantages. It can store two 8-bit bytes. The byte has become a virtually standard unit of measure since IBM standardized on it and on EBCDIC (Extended Binary Coded Decimal Interchange Code) when the System/360 was introduced in 1964. Storage capacity and requirements are measured in bytes. Computer peripherals and data communications equipment handle bytes of data. Thus, for compatibility with the rest of the computer industry, minicomputers must be able to handle bytes, and the 16-bit word does this nicely.

The 16-bit word is long enough to allow enough code combinations for a reasonable size of instruction set, with bits left over to address a substantial part of memory directly, typically 256 to 1024 words. The 16-bit word is short enough to permit relatively simple and inexpensive control logic. Internal registers for buffering (temporary storage) of data and control words are relatively short in comparison to those of large computers where data words are often 32 bits long and control words 64 bits long (IBM System/360).

Minicomputers can handle data that will not fit into the 16-word bit by using software subroutines or hardware options that treat two or more words as a unit. Double precision (two-word), fixed-point arithmetic routines and multiple precision (two- to four-words) floating-point arithmetic routines are supplied with the system software for applications requiring greater precision than the 16-bit word provides. Software subroutines are much slower than hardware implementation, by factors ranging from the tens to hundreds.

Minicomputers can address all locations in memory but not directly from the instruction word. For this, they need other addressing methods that use an additional word for direct, indirect, or index addressing.

Because many minicomputer applications do not require much arithmetic capability, the basic processor often implements only "add" and "subtract" in the hardware; some implement only "add" and "complement," and subtraction must be done by complementing the subtrahend and adding it to the minuend. Software subroutines are supplied for "multiply" and "divide." Most offer multiply/divide hardware as an option. Larger minicomputer systems also offer optional floating-point hardware for applications that require it.

Initially, minicomputer manufacturers could avoid costly outlays for software development because the specialized programming needs of dedicated applications did not require extensive system software. Typical software provided with a minicomputer system include a compiler (FORTRAN, BASIC, or ALGOL), an assembler, a small set of utilities, and a modest operating system. As minicomputer manufacturers began to address more complex applications, such as real-time control combined with batch processing and time sharing, however, the development of extensive system software became not only practical but also essential for user acceptance.

Although minicomputer software is increasing in sophistication, applicable operating systems are considerably less sophisticated than those for large scale systems, such as EXEC 8 for the Univac 1100 Series and OS for the IBM systems 360 and 370. These operating systems can handle a large variety of problems, but they have cost hundreds of thousands or even millions of dollars to develop. Also, all large-scale systems support the COBOL language for programming commercial data processing problems; some also support the PL/1 (Programming Language 1), which has combined features from COBOL, FORTRAN, and ALGOL. Compilers to translate COBOL programs into machine-language code require large quantities of main memory and are very expensive to develop, costing a half-million dollars or more. No minicomputer supports a full COBOL compiler.

Operating systems for minicomputers tend to be specialized for one kind of processing, such as real time, time sharing, or batch. Also, they tend to offer fewer systems. Time-sharing operating systems for example, generally are for desk calculator operations and use only one language, such as BASIC or FOCAL.

MINICOMPUTER APPLICATIONS

Despite the minicomputer's relatively short history, it has already been successfully used in a wide range of applications, both as a stand-alone general-purpose system and for specialized dedicated functions.

Scope of Present Markets

Minicomputers are sold extensively OEM, as mentioned earlier. They are commonly used as the central element of industrial process control systems and intelligent terminals. They also operate as components of large computer systems or networks and function as front-end communications processors. In some cases, they function as peripheral processors for the large computers. In hierarchal computer systems where responsibilities are shared among a group of computers, a number of minicomputers can be used to perform different functions within the overall system (Fig. 1-3).

Minicomputers have penetrated existing markets, such as time sharing, and they have created new markets, such as laboratory experiment monitoring. Despite the broad view of minicomputer markets, most are installed in dedicated applications, sold to OEMs, or used in markets closed to larger, more costly computers. A frequent application is as a desk calculator for a design engineer or laboratory experimenter.

Generally, minicomputers are not appropriate for applications that require a large data base or complex I/O operations. Because their memories are relatively small, they cannot store the large operating systems needed to control such systems efficiently.

Utilization

The minicomputer, as is its larger counterpart, is used in two basic ways, as a controller and as a calculator/data processor. Minicomputers are used to control (1) processes, such as those encountered in a chemical plant or an experimental laboratory (Fig. 1-4); (2) devices, such as typesetting machines or optical character readers; and (3) transfer of data, as in a data communications network. They are also used as calculators to solve complex scientific problems, perform business data processing (Fig. 1-5), and even solve students' homework problems.

The greatest advantage the minicomputer has over larger computers is that the user need buy only the system hardware required to perform a specific task. A larger computer, used for the same application, would typically have excess capacity and power that are wasted. As can any general-purpose computer, the minicomputer can perform any task for which

FIG. 1-3.   Data General Corporation—A system with eight interconnected Nova 800 computers; 155,648 words of core memory, and almost 5 million words of disk storage.

it can be programmed. Unlike the large machines, which are typically centrally located and remote from the user, the minicomputer is usually a personal computer; it is installed close to the user, who has easy access to it.

This tendency to put minicomputers "where the action is" stems from their small size and ruggedness (Figure 1-6). They need no air conditioning or special flooring; most are compact enough to squeeze into a few square feet of floor space.

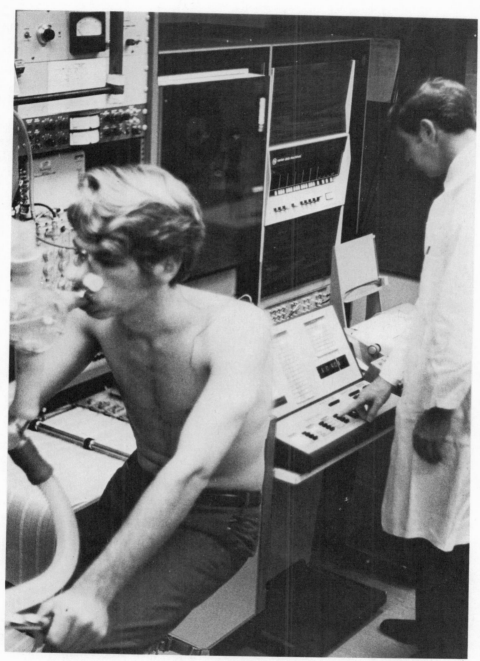

FIG. 1-4.   Varian Data Machines 620/i minicomputer-based system for testing cardio-pulmonary and exercise physiology functions.

FIG. 1-5.   DEC DATASYSTEM-520—A stand-alone general-purpose small business computer built around the PDP-11.

Application Areas

In this book, minicomputer applications are grouped into five general areas, characterized by the function performed and the resultant design requirements. Of these application areas, industrial control has been prevalent and has accounted for over 40 percent of minicomputer system sales. Communication and computation are also important applications and are projected to increase in importance. A detailed expansion of these application areas is given in Appendix F.

LIMITATIONS

Minicomputers do have drawbacks. Until recently, few systems came with extensive system software, which made them difficult to program. This problem has been rapidly overcome as manufacturers have developed

FIG. 1-6. IBM System 17—Where the action is—small, fast, rugged, and can communicate with 1130, 1800, and System/360.

compiler languages and operating systems for their machines and have designed specialized application packages for market segments broad enough to amortize the software development costs.

A second drawback is that conventional computer peripherals such as line printers, magnetic tape units, card readers and punches, and disks are

Table 1-1. General Areas of Minicomputer Use

APPLICATION AREA	FUNCTIONAL DESCRIPTION
Industrial control	Controls continuous industrial processes in the chemical, petroleum, food processing, utility, and other industries.
	Controls the operation of numerically controlled machine tools.
	Controls a variety of special industrial operations like type-setting in the publishing industry or automatic system testing in the electronics industry.
Peripheral control	Controls the operation of other equipment, such as computer output microfilm, optical character readers, key-to-tape and key-to-disk computer input systems, digital plotters, line printers, magnetic tape units, magnetic disk units, and intelligent terminals.
Communications	Controls the concentration of data from several low-speed communications lines onto one high-speed line.
	Controls the flow of messages in message switching systems.
	Controls the transfer of data between a large computer and communication lines connected to remote terminals.
Computation	Used as the central processor in a free-standing computer system performing general business data processing functions.
	Used as the central processor in a free-standing computer system performing scientific computations.
	Used as the central processor in small in-house time-sharing systems.
Data acquisition	Controls the operation of scientific experiments and instruments.
	Monitors various types of experiments or operations to accumulate performance data.

expensive relative to the minicomputer central processor cost. Line printers that typically cost $30,000 to $40,000 and magnetic tape units that cost $20,000 to $30,000 cannot be considered peripheral to a minicomputer system that costs $10,000 to $15,000. Until 1969, minicomputer users either did without conventional peripherals or bought peripherals not scaled to their systems.

Since 1969, a host of peripherals scaled to minicomputer systems have appeared on the market. Today, most major minicomputer systems can be configured with a large selection of conventional peripherals. Manufacturers have had notable success in reducing the cost of card readers, paper tape devices, line printers, disks, and magnetic tape drives. Disk prices have dropped markedly, and most minicomputers can support both fixed-head disks for system software storage and movable-head disk packs or cartridges for data file storage. Magnetic tape cassettes have been developed for storing modest amounts of data at low cost. Card punches, on the other hand, are seldom supplied because their cost is still high. Although significant progress has been made, more low-cost peripherals are needed.

Minicomputers also have certain fundamental drawbacks such as short word lengths, limited instruction sets, small memories, and limited I/O capabilities. The increasingly flexible software provided with minicomputers does overcome these shortcomings in the sense that the user does not have to worry about them. Memory size has increased to 64K bytes for most systems and to 132K or 264K bytes for larger minicomputers. The I/O limitations remain, however, despite such options as direct memory access, because most minicomputers have only one memory bus, which must be time shared by the processor and the I/O channels. As a practical matter, system throughput is limited by the memory cycle time, even though cycle time has dropped markedly as core memories have become faster and semiconductor solid-state memories have become generally available.

Some minicomputer systems interleave memory modules to allow faster memory access times, and use multiple memory buses to allow simultaneous memory accesses to different memory modules. These features increase system throughput but increase system cost.

Maintenance presents further problems to users. Many manufacturers offer local service only to large urban areas or provide a small number of maintenance centers. Therefore, users in distant areas must stock spare parts and perform most of the necessary maintenance themselves. When a minicomputer is only a component in a system produced by another company, the user's contact with the minicomputer manufacturer is tenuous. On the other hand, the reliability of minicomputers has been good. Circuit boards (Fig. 1-7) are generally repaired only at the manufacturer's home plant, and in-the-field maintenance mainly consists of plugging in a new circuit board.

MINICOMPUTER COSTS

Most minicomputers are purchased. Manufacturers who produce minicomputers exclusively do not lease their systems. Some do have plans whereby a separate lending agency lends money to a user to purchase a

FIG. 1-7.   Data General Corporation 8K-word core memory unit on a single circuit board.

system. Third parties also lease some systems. Large companies, such as IBM, Honeywell, and Xerox, which produce large computers as well as minicomputers, do lease their minicomputers. When leased, the monthly rental includes maintenance. Monthly rental for a one-year lease ranges from about 2 to 2.9 percent of the purchase price. About 14 to 25 percent of the monthly rental is for maintenance. For purchased systems, maintenance varies from 1 to 3.5 percent of the purchase price.

How much does a minicomputer cost? The price varies, depending on the number of features included in the basic system. Most systems are modular, so a user can buy specifically what he needs without any excess features. A Texas Instruments TI 960 A with 4096 words of semiconductor memory costs $2850. A DEC PDP-11 with 4096 words of memory, a programmer's console, and Teletype ASR 33 with control costs $10,800. An IBM System 7 with 2048 words of memory costs $8500. These are very different systems; each has characteristics and interface capabilities that might very well make one or the other a better buy for a particular application.

Generally, the cost of a minicomputer system purchased from a large computer manufacturer is higher than one purchased from a minicomputer manufacturer. Their markup is higher because of their larger sales and support organizations. Whether the large computer manufacturer does provide more needed user support is questionable. To date, most mini-computer users are relatively sophisticated and do not require elementary help.

Because minicomputers are designed modularly on plug-in LSI (large-scale integration) circuit boards, and repairs to the board are usually done only at the factory, maintenance consists in many cases of plugging in a new board. Users can stock spare boards and plug in a new one themselves. Furthermore, minicomputers have proved their reliability. This does not mean that maintenance arrangements should not be considered. What it means is that maintenance is not the problem it was a few years ago. Using air travel, a maintenance man located quite far away can be on site in a matter of hours to most places.

Furthermore, the cost of the mainframe is only a part of the total system cost. Peripherals, interfacing, software, and operating costs can quickly overshadow it.

SUMMARY

Although minicomputers and large-scale computers are similar in many ways, minicomputers do have characteristics that distinguish them from large general-purpose computers. Minicomputers are small, inexpensive, and personal. Both outright purchase and leasing offer advantages to such financial considerations as amortization, depreciation, maintenance, and operating costs. They are very modular, with the basic system containing the minimum hardware required for data processing of any kind. Many optional features are available to tailor a system to a user's specific application. Generally, minicomputers are unsuitable for applications requiring a large data base or high I/O rates, which characterize most large commercial processing jobs.

2. MINICOMPUTER MAINFRAME ARCHITECTURE AND MEMORY

Just as the minicomputer industry has evolved from the larger EDP industry, so minicomputer design has evolved from that of larger computers. Minicomputer systems are conceptually identical to bigger systems, and can be similarly divided into a mainframe, peripheral equipment, and software. The block diagram in Figure 2-1 illustrates the components and organization of a typical minicomputer system.

MAINFRAME

The <u>mainframe</u> or <u>central processor</u> of a minicomputer system contains the basic computer logic, internal memory, and control. It consists of the following logical units:

Arithmetic unit: Performs the arithmetic operations required to process data (add, complement, shift, delete, compare).

Control unit: Sequences operations, decodes instructions, and provides the control signals to coordinate the actions of the arithmetic unit, memory, and the input/output devices (I/O) to execute the instructions.

Main memory: Stores and retrieves instructions and data in response to control signals from the control unit or I/O control.

Input/output control: Transfers information between the computer or memory and I/O devices in response to signals from the control unit and the external peripheral devices.

16

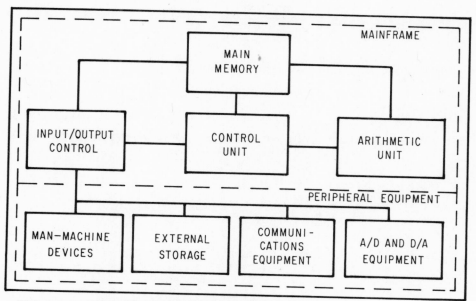

FIG. 2-1.   Block diagram of a typical minicomputer system.

The central processor and the main memory largely determine the computing power of a computer system. The most important processor characteristics are instruction set; addressing capabilities; instruction execution speed; the number, size, and arrangement of accumulators and/or index registers; the number of interrupts and method of handling them; the I/O structure and optional features. Important main memory characteristics are word length, cycle time, and size (number of words stored).

The size, power, and relevance to the user's application of the machine's instruction set determine how rapidly and easily the problem can be programmed. A programmer can overcome the absence of a desired instruction by using several simpler instructions, but this requires more programming effort, occupies more space in main memory, and lengthens program running time.

Addressing capability depends on the instruction word length, the processor logic, and the memory size. In general, the limited number of bits available in the instruction word for the operand address mandates that some addressing technique such as indexing, indirect addressing, or paging be used to address all of main memory. Instruction execution speed depends on memory cycle time as well as the computer's internal logic.

The number, size, and arrangement of accumulators and index registers affect programming ease and flexibility as well as execution efficiency. Generally, the more accumulators and index registers available, the easier the computer is to program, the faster programs will run, and the less memory required to store a program. The number of interrupts a computer can handle is a major factor in its applicability to process control systems. External devices use the interrupt system to monitor process conditions and to communicate these conditions to the processor. The more interrupts the system can handle quickly and efficiently, the more complex the control system can be.

A priority interrupt system allows the organization of external events into hierarchies according to the need of the overall system. Time-critical events or alarm conditions are given highest priority; thus, they communicate with the processor via the highest-priority interrupt lines. The processor suspends the execution of all other program until these critical conditions are taken care of. Less time-critical external events can be interfaced to lower priority lines in the order of their time requirements. In other words, an event that requires servicing by the processor within 10 ms (milliseconds) of its occurrence is connected to an interrupt line of higher priority than the interrupt line used for an event that requires servicing within 10 seconds.

Optional features, such as power fail/safe, built-in timers, and memory protection, are essential for many applications, especially in process control, time sharing, and data communications. A power fail/safe device delays system shutdown and gives the processor time to store the internal registers in nonvolatile core memory, to switch to a standby duplicate system in some instances, or to switch to battery power before the system goes down. Saving the contents of internal registers makes it possible to restart computing when power is restored. For some applications, system shutdown has disastrous consequences. For example, a control system for a chemical, power, or sewage disposal plant cannot be allowed to shut down. For these applications, duplicate minicomputers programmed in the same way are often used; they alternate in controlling the system and in standing by. In addition, a standby power supply is used in case of power failure.

Semiconductor memory is volatile, that is, its contents will be destroyed if power fails. Core memory is nonvolatile; it will hold its contents indefinitely if power fails. Most manufacturers who build minicomputers with semiconductor memory will supply batteries for alternate memory power if main power fails.

Timers are needed for applications where the computer must be synchronized with real-time events, devices that operate at different speeds, and data communication lines. Timers are also used to allocate computer time to various users at intervals. For example, time-sharing systems allot computing time to the users on a round-robin basis, such as 1 ms for each in turn. Frequently, in control systems, processes are done at fixed time intervals.

Memory protection provides a boundary between memory locations that are protected and those that are not. Generally, the operating system and real-time programs that control processes are stored in protected memory so that undebugged programs cannot inadvertently destroy them. Some operating systems confine each user program to a specific area of memory so that one user program cannot interfere with any other user program. When memory is protected, the processor examines each address generated by the user program and signals an interrupt if any address is in the protected memory area.

Mainframe Architecture

Mainframe architecture is the fundamental internal design of the machine. Most manufacturers design their minicomputers as general-purpose systems so that they can be used for a broad range of applications. Yet, certain minicomputers are better than others for a particular application. This is so because nobody has proved that a particular design is the optimum for general-purpose processing. Even if an optimum design were found, however, a manufacturer could decide to design a minicomputer to do general-purpose processing moderately well but to be a whiz at data communication applications. He would do this because his marketing strategy was planned to concentrate on data communication applications. Another manufacturer might concentrate on process control, another on scientific processing, and another on time sharing.

Other factors enter into design decisions: the cost of implementing different features, trade-offs among cost, speed, and flexibility, and compatibility with other systems.

Some features are expensive to implement. One of these is floating-point arithmetic, which is infrequently used for many applications but is essential for some applications. Thus, floating-point arithmetic hardware is a perfect example of a feature that should be optional and priced separately. Those who need it, buy it; those who do not need it, do not buy it. That is a relatively simple decision, but if a user needs it, how elegant should the floating-point arithmetic hardware be? Should it have instructions for using two-word, three-word, or four-word operands, or all of them? Should it have instructions to convert from fixed point to floating point, and vice versa? Should it be able to compare floating-point operands? Various manufacturers make these decisions in different ways, depending on marketing and cost.

Trade-offs among costs, speed, and flexibility can be complex. To illustrate, let us examine the case for and against a microprogrammed processor. In the past, few minicomputers were microprogrammed, but today many are. The conventional way to implement computer logic for addition, for example, was to design a circuit to add two numbers together and treat this circuit as a logic unit. Other instructions could be designed to reuse this logic unit, if part of the instruction required it. If only pieces of the add circuit were required, however, a separate circuit was designed for that instruction. This is an oversimplification of the process, since designers did strive to organize the logic so as to avoid circuit duplication as much as possible.

Microprogramming formalized this procedure of searching for small logic units that could be used over and over again. A microprogrammed processor divides the computer logic into small logic units, which are controlled by microinstruction words stored in binary form in a read-only memory. Each bit in the microinstruction word controls a circuit that implements a logical operation, which might be OUTPUT THE CONTENTS OF REGISTER A TO INTERNAL BUS. By setting up the appropriate combination of one or more bits in microinstruction words, a complex operation can be performed.

A computer instruction, such as ADD (from memory to register A), is used to select (jump to) the memory location in read-only memory, where the microinstructions are stored, to implement ADD. Because computer logic consists of quite a number of basic logic elements, microinstruction words tend to be longer than main memory words; they are commonly 32 to 64 bits long.

The primary advantage of microprogrammed processors is their flexibility. Manufacturers can change the technology implementing the basic logic elements without redesigning microprograms. Conversely, microprograms can be changed to implement a different instruction set without changing the processor design. This is especially useful for emulating an older system for which programs have been written. In fact, the processor can operate like any other processor if a microprogram has been written for it and the read-only memory board has been built.

Interdata's minicomputers (Fig. 2-2) have always been microprogrammed, and as far back as 1967 the company allowed users to specify what they wanted in their instruction set. Interdata then wired up the circuits of the read-only memory board to implement the required data instructions. The user plugged in the board and had his own specialized computer.

Some manufacturers, notably Hewlett-Packard, Varian Data Machines, and Interdata, have now gone even further and use writable control stores (Fig. 2-3), which operate like the older read-only microprogrammed memories except that the contents of the writable control stores can now be

FIG. 2-2. Interdata family of compatible minicomputer processors. Front row—Model 74 (left), Model 70 (right); Middle row—Model 80 (left), Model 50 (right); Back row—Model 70 with INTERTAPE cassette (left), Model 55 (right), prototypes of two unannounced systems (middle).

changed by the programmer under certain conditions. These writable control stores can be used in two ways: to add special-purpose instructions to the standard instruction set, or to implement a completely new instruction set. The user pays a price if he changes the standard instruction set because the system software supports only the standard set. It is useful, however, to implement frequently used subroutines, which are treated as instructions by the computer but are treated as subroutines by the software.

A hardwired processor with the same components as a microprogrammed processor is faster because the microprogrammed processor must access the control store memory each time a microinstruction is executed. A computer instruction may require the execution of several microinstructions and thus the memory-access times add up. On the other hand, control memories are four, five, or more times faster than most main memories—100 to 200 ns (nanoseconds) as compared to 750 to 1000 ns.

FIG. 2-3.   Hewlett Packard—Plug-in card adds writable control store to the
HP-2100 computer.

A <u>microprogrammed processor</u> has many advantages. Optional features
can be added by plugging in more control memory boards. Different processor models can use the same basic hardwired design even though each has
a different control store. A new system can easily emulate an older system
and use its software. Despite these advantages, all manufacturers do not
use microprogrammed logic for all their systems because faster processors
can be made with hardwired logic. Also, very high speed control store
memories are expensive.

In many cases, a newly announced processor is a redesigned version of
an older processor. The new version may incorporate new technology that
improves the price/performance ratio (usually faster and cheaper), but
to the software and the user it operates like the old machine. Because time
and money have been invested to develop software for the old system, the
manufacturer does not want to lose that investment. Digital Equipment,

for example, has redesigned the PDP-8 a number of times. This is not surprising because the PDP-8 is the most popular minicomputer ever built and still outsells all others each year. The PDP-8 has a limited instruction set, has no index registers, and uses a 12-bit word. The system software is so extensive, however, that a user is not hampered by its internal design.

Other manufacturers, who also have a large customer base and have heavy investments in system software, make their new systems compatible with or able to emulate older systems. The Varian Data Machines' Varian 73 can emulate the older 620 line. The Hewlett-Packard HP-2100A (Fig. 2-4) can emulate the HP-2116. The Honeywell System 700 is upward compatible with the Series 16 line.

Along with redesigned machines, manufacturers do introduce minicomputer models with new architectures as well as new technology. Digital Equipment's PDP-11 and Hewlett-Packard's HP-3000 are two such systems. They incorporate features that make system software programming and peripheral interfacing easier. Neither system was made to be compatible with any other computer, and thus the designers were free to incorporate new architecture.

Thus, the mainframe architecture for the most popular minicomputers on the market today varies considerably depending on the constraints placed on the logical designers.

Data Structure

Data formats are usually expressed in relationship to processor word length. Word length consists of the number of bits treated as a unit throughout the system. Because words are handled as a unit, the number of bits per word determines the number of parallel hardware units required for such things as lines in a data path and flip-flops to store bits in internal registers.

One or more parity bits are added to each word if memory parity checking is offered. Sometimes one parity bit is added per word. Sometimes a bit is added for each 8-bit byte; thus, two parity bits are added to a 16-bit word and three to a 24-bit word. Parity bits are added to words written in memory to make all number 1s in a word an odd number. For example, if a word made up of an even number of 1s were stored in memory, a 1 would be written into a parity bit to make the number of bits odd. If the word contained an odd number of 1s, a zero would be written into the parity bit to leave the number of 1s odd. When words are read from memory, the 1s in each word are added to determine if the sum is odd. If the number is even, a memory parity error-interrupt is signaled.

The 8-, 16-, and 24-bit word processors are most compatible with data

FIG. 2-4.   Hewlett-Packard Model 2120A disk operating system with 2100A
computer and 7900A moving-head disk provides twice the on-line storage of its
predecessors.

formats used by the rest of the computer industry, which generally expresses data formats in terms of the 8-bit byte because this word size is an
integral number of bytes in length. Processors that use an 8-bit word gen-

erally require two words for operands and instructions; thus, in many respects they are similar to those that use a 16-bit word. The 12-bit and 18-bit processors in use today are descendants of processor lines that predate the standardization of the byte or were designed to be compatible with an older line.

Instructions are generally one, two, or three words long. The first word contains the operation (instruction code) field and an addressing field, which can usually address a small portion of memory. The second and third words, if used, are for addressing all of memory (see the later section "Addressing").

Operands for fixed-point arithmetic (ADD, SUBTRACT, MULTIPLY, and DIVIDE) are generally one word long. Some processors also have some instructions that can use half-word (byte for 16-bit words) or two-word operands.

Floating-point arithmetic operands are generally two, three, or four words long. The first word holds the sign of the fraction, the exponent (generally expressed in excess 64 or 128 code), and the most significant seven or eight bits of the fraction. The remaining words store the less significant fraction bits.

The exponent is generally stored in excess code to avoid storing a sign for the exponent. In excess code, a zero is expressed as a positive integer; positive and negative exponents are expressed in relationship to it. For example, in excess-64 code, a zero is expressed as 64, a one is 65, two is 66, and so on; a minus one is 63, a minus two is 62, a minus three is 61, and so on. Excess codes are used for the convenience of programmers; they do not save on the number of bits required to store numbers within a fixed range.

Internal Registers

Most processors are designed around a group of internal registers, some of which are programmable while others are not. The nonprogrammable registers operate as buffers that hold a word temporarily for the processor hardware. The types of registers are:

1. An instruction register holds the instruction word while the instruction is being executed.

2. A memory address register holds the memory address while a word is being read from or written into memory.

3. One or two memory data registers hold the word read from or written into memory.

4. A program counter register holds the address of the next instruction to be executed.

The programmable registers also operate as buffers and provide temporary storage of words for the program. These registers may comprise one or more accumulators that hold operands for arithmetic, logic, or transfer operations. One of the accumulators is usually the primary one; it always holds one operand and usually receives the result of an operation. One or more of the programmable index registers is used as base addresses for addressing memory.

Some processors, particularly those with the most modern architecture, have multiple general-purpose internal registers (8 to 16); they can be used as accumulators, as stack pointers for stack processing, or as index registers. Sometimes the program counter is a dedicated general-purpose register and can be programmed in the same way as other general-purpose registers.

Instruction Set

All the operations a user can program into the computer to do in machine language codes comprise the instruction set. Assemblers and compilers of higher-level languages, such as FORTRAN or ALGOL, incorporate pseudo-instructions (those that direct the assembler or compiler) and macro-instructions (those that perform a function, usually a processing function) that effectively extend the instruction set as far as the user is concerned. The pseudo- and macro-instructions, however, are implemented by executing a number of machine language instructions for each pseudo- or macro-instruction executed. The true instruction set consists of the machine language instructions only.

The large number of instructions in the instruction set is often cited as an asset for a computer. It can be an asset if the right kind of instructions are implemented, but usually the large number is derived by counting every minor variation of the instruction rather than counting only the general instructions. For example, the SHIFT instruction, which moves the operand one bit position to the right, may comprise five or six instructions in a list because the operand can be located in one of a number of different internal registers.

Most minicomputers use a one-word instruction format with 4 to 6 bits assigned as the instruction code; the other 10 to 12 bits (assuming the common 16-bit word) are used for addressing. Additional instruction words, if used, generally contain base addresses for extending the number of memory locations that can be addressed.

If the operation code is only four bits long, it appears that the processor can have only 16 instructions ($2^4 = 16$). To get around this limitation, 14 of these codes are generally used for instructions that address memory; one code signals an I/O operation and the other code signals an internal register operation. The I/O and register instructions then use the bits in the address field to define which I/O or register operation is performed. This increases the number of instruction codes available so that hundreds of instructions can be defined.

To increase the number of instructions that can address memory, the operation code field must be increased. If it is increased to 5 bits, 30 codes can be used for instructions that address memory. If 6 bits are used for the operation code, 62 codes can be used for instructions that address memory.

Classes of Instructions   Instruction sets for minicomputers include six or more classes of instructions:

Load/Store: Transfers words of data between the internal registers and memory. Some can transfer words between memory locations directly without using an internal register. Some can also transfer half-words (bytes) or bits.

Fixed-point arithmetic: Minimum includes add, two's complement or one's complement and add one, and shift or rotate one bit to the left or right. Most include add, subtract, two's complement and shift. Multiply and divide can be standard or optional instructions. Single precision (one-word) operands are usually standard. Double precision (two-word) operands are sometimes optional. Half-word (byte) operands can sometimes be used for add and subtract. Multiple shifts and multiple rotate are sometimes optional.

Floating-point arithmetic: Almost universally optional if available at all. Add, subtract, multiply, and divide using two-word operands are most common. Some also have instructions for four-word operands: to normalize, to convert between fixed and floating-point formats, and to compare.

Logic: AND, OR, and exclusive OR are most common.

Control: Most common are compare; skip if equal, not equal, less than, greater than, or zero; unconditional jump; conditional jump; test and skip if set or reset. Some use I/O instructions to control memory protect, memory relocate, interrupt, and other optional features.

I/O: Transfers one word between I/O device and processor (can be data, control, or status word). Meaning of control and status words depends on the device. Some treat optional features as I/O devices and use I/O instructions to control them.

Others: Some specialized processors compute trigonometric functions, such as tangent, sine, square root.

To date, only one minicomputer (the Lockheed Electronics SUE 1112) has decimal arithmetic instructions as a standard feature. The SUE uses a microprogrammed processor and implements its instructions using a microprogrammed control memory. As microprogrammed processors become more prevalent and users and manufacturers gain more experience in microprogramming and its uses, many specialized instruction sets will be offered with systems as optional features. The current stumbling block is the problem of coordinating specialized instruction sets with the system software supported by the manufacturer. Generally, the manufacturer's software supports only the standard instruction set, and users who microprogram specialized instruction sets must develop all their own software. This is not feasible for any user except a system house that produces specialized systems for the end-user market.

Stack processing is a recent addition to minicomputer facilities. Stack processing, like byte and bit manipulation facilities, is implemented primarily through the addressing structure rather than the instruction set.

Addressing

Most minicomputers use one-address instructions (that is, an instruction can address only one main memory location); thus, only one operand can be located in main memory. The other operand is understood to be located in an internal register called an "accumulator." The result of the operation is always placed back in the accumulator or in the main memory location.

For systems with multiple accumulators or general-purpose registers, the instruction word provides for specifying the register that will operate as the accumulator as well as the address of the operand located in main memory. The result is placed in the accumulator or back in main memory.

The small number of bits in the instruction word allotted to the address field for most minicomputers limits the number of memory locations that can be directly addressed by the instruction. For the most common 16-bit word length and a minimum size operation code of four bits, a maximum of 12 bits remains in the instruction word to address memory; 12 bits can address only 4096 locations. For systems with maximum memory sizes of 32K, 64K, or 128K words (K = 1024 in computer jargon), means other than direct addressing must be used to address all of memory.

The oldest and commonest addressing techniques are direct, immediate absolute, relative, indirect, and indexed addressing. For these techniques, part of the address field (for example, 3 bits) selects the addressing technique or mode and the rest of the field (9 bits) operates as an address, an address displacement, or an operand. It is also unused sometimes, depending on the addressing mode.

Of all the addressing modes listed, immediate addressing is not really addressing at all; the address field is treated as an operand. This is useful for generating constants needed for setting up counters, adding increments, or generating initial parameters for mathematical expressions. In our example, 9-bit constants can be specified. Some systems can also generate full-word constants (16-bits for our example). In this case, the word following the instruction word is usually treated as a constant, and the instruction is effectively two words long.

For direct addressing, the address field is used as the operand address. For our example, the 9-bit displacement can address only the first 512 locations in main memory.

Absolute addressing differs from direct addressing in that it does not use the displacement field at all; instead, the word following the instruction word is used as the operand address. Using the 16-bit word example, 65,536 memory locations can be addressed.

Relative Addressing   Relative addressing is a simple technique for extending the addressing range; the address is calculated relative to the content of the program counter, which points to the address of the next instruction to be executed. The most significant bit of the address displacement is usually treated as a sign bit, so memory locations below and above the one containing the instruction can be addressed. Because the content of the program counter is incremented each time an instruction is executed, the block of memory locations the instruction word can address changes as the program progresses; one location is added at the top of the block and one is dropped from the bottom for each instruction executed. Again we use the example of the 9-bit displacement field, with the most significant bit treated as a sign. Each instruction word can address 256 locations above the one containing the instruction word and 255 locations below it.

Using relative addressing throughout a program has one inherent advantage. The program can run without alteration no matter where it is located in main memory. This is very useful in multiprogramming applications where a number of different programs are running concurrently at different times and programs are being loaded into whatever memory space is available.

Indirect Addressing   Indirect addressing is another common addressing technique. In this case the displacement field in the instruction word is treated as the address of a memory location that contains not an operand but the operand address. The instruction word can address a limited number of locations that can contain operand addresses, which can address any location in memory. In our example of the 9-bit address displacement, the instruction word can address the first 512 memory locations in memory. These locations contain 16-bit words, which can address 65,536 memory locations.

Indirect addressing is often recursive; that is, an indirect address can specify another indirect address. To do this, one bit of the indirect address is treated as a control bit, which specifies whether the other bits are to be used as the operand address or as another indirect address. For the 16-bit word computer, the indirect address would now contain only 15 bits, so it could address 32,768 memory locations.

Generally, programs using long indirect addressing chains are discouraged by the manufacturers. Each indirect address requires a memory access and lengthens instruction execution time by one memory cycle time. Usually the processor accepts interrupts only after an instruction has been completely executed, and long indirect addressing chains lock out interrupts and degrade the processors' response time to interrupts. Also, programs with long, indirect addressing chains are hard to debug.

Indirect addressing also has an inherent advantage. It allows a subroutine to return to the program that used it without knowing where that program is located in memory. Subroutines are programmed to return to the main program by way of an indirect address in a specific memory location or internal register. The main program loads that location with the content of the program counter as it jumps to the subroutine. Most minicomputers have an instruction to do this automatically, which is usually called something like JUMP TO SUBROUTINE AND STORE RETURN.

Indexed Addressing   Another common addressing technique is indexed addressing. In this case, the address field is treated as a displacement relative to the content of an index register. The index register can be an internal register or a dedicated main memory location. Because of the time required to access main memory, most of today's minicomputers implement index registers as internal registers. As a holdover from the days when index registers were dedicated memory locations, some index registers are addressed as memory locations but are actually internal registers. This is done to gain the speed of an internal register and to maintain compatibility with older systems. Honeywell, for example, does this with its System 700, which is upward compatible with its older, popular Series 16 line.

The trend is toward more index registers, with part of the address field in the instruction word devoted to selecting the index register. Multiple index registers cut down on the number of instructions required to program a problem; consequently they reduce program execution time and the amount of memory required to store a program. If a system has only one index register, it must be loaded and stored over and over again as the program uses it for different purposes, such as for loop (section of code used repetitively) control and for addressing operands.

Indexed addressing is similar to relative addressing except that the content of an index register rather than the program counter is used as the base address. For the example of the 9-bit displacement field and one index register, the instruction word can address a block of 512 memory locations relative to the index register content. If the displacement is treated as a positive number, 512 locations beyond the base address in the index register. If the displacement is treated as a signed number, 255 locations above and below the base address in the index register can be addressed. For a 16-bit word, it can address 65,536 words.

Suppose a system has three index registers; then 2 bits of the 9-bit displacement field must be used to select the index register. This leaves a 7-bit displacement, which can address any location within a block of 128 words relative to the three base addresses located in the index register.

Most systems use variations and combinations of direct, immediate, absolute, relative, indirect, and indexed addressing. Usually, two or more modes can be combined in one instruction word, such as relative indirect, indexed indirect, relative indexed, and relative indexed indirect. Pre-indexing means indexing is done before indirect addressing; post-indexing means indexing done after all indirect addressing.

Auto-indexing   Digital Equipment has implemented auto-indexing on its PDP-8. A block of eight memory locations in each 4K-word increment or field of main memory operates in a special way. They operate in the same way as other memory locations except in indirect address; then the content is incremented by one before it is used as the operand address. Data General has two 8-word blocks of memory locations that operate as auto-increment or auto-decrement registers on the Nova/Supernova computers. When indirectly addressed, a location in one of the 8-word blocks increments its content before it is used as the operand address; a location in the other 8-word group decrements its content before it is used as the operand address.

Byte and Bit Addressing   For addressing purposes, some 16-bit word processors operate as if memory were composed of 8-bit bytes. The address calculated by the instruction word is treated as a half-word or byte address. The operation code specifies whether the instruction is to use byte or word operands. The least significant bit of the calculated address specifies which half-word or byte is to be used. Because memory is actually composed of 16-bit words, word-addressing instructions must always calculate an address that specifies the most significant byte and least significant bit "0." Otherwise, a word instruction would specify bytes from two different physical word locations, and this is not allowed.

Byte addressing is very useful for I/O operations because many devices transfer bytes of data, and data from I/O devices can be easily packed with two bytes per word as it is read from an input device. The reverse is also easy to do. Characters stored two per word can be unpacked and transferred one character at a time to an output device.

A few minicomputers that have been designed primarily for process control applications can also address bits within a word. Usually, the operation code specifies that the instruction is to use bit addressing, and the address field specifies which bit in the word. The address of the memory location that contains the word is either in an internal register or in the memory location following the instruction. Texas Instrument's TI960A can go even further; it can address variable-length fields of bits within a word for one of its I/O instructions.

Bit addressing is useful for control applications because many signals to and from noncomputer process control instruments are two-valued; for example, TEST FOR SWITCH ON/OFF, TURN VALVE ON/OFF. A control system can be supervising many such devices as well as performing calculations, taking readings, and making log reports; so it is a definite plus if the processor can handle bits efficiently.

PDP-11 Addressing   Up to 1970, when Digital Equipment introduced its PDP-11, minicomputers used variations or combinations of the addressing techniques just described. The PDP-11 architecture is radically different from that of earlier minicomputers, particularly in its addressing facilities. Because these addressing facilities are conceptually simple and superior to those offered with other systems, minicomputer manufacturers will undoubtedly reflect on the PDP-11 as they design new systems. Good old American ingenuity combined with the restraints of the patent laws may produce interesting variations on the PDP-11 addressing, but its influence will shine through.

First of all the PDP-11 is a 16-bit word computer. Instructions are one, two, or three words long, and an instruction specifies two addresses if an operation requires two operands. Both operands can be located in main memory; both can be in internal registers; or one can be in an internal register and the other in main memory. The result can be stored either in main memory or in an internal register.

Second, the PDP-11 has no direct addressing facilities, as defined earlier; that is, it does not have a main memory address in the instruction word. All addressing is done through eight internal general purpose registers.

(The PDP-11/40 and 11/45 have 9 and 16, respectively, but addressing is the same for all models. See Appendix A for a PDP-11 summary.) The internal registers are 16-bits long; thus they can address 65,536 memory locations. Addressing is to the byte level, so 32,768 memory words can be addressed. The instruction word for two-operand instructions uses a 4-bit operation code and two 6-bit address fields, a source address field, and a destination address field. The result is stored in the location specified by the destination field. Each address field consists of a 3-bit address mode and a 3-bit register address. The source address is calculated first and the destination address second. Each address is generated in two steps. The first step uses two bits of the address mode field to calculate a basic address. The third bit then specifies whether the basic address is used directly or is used as an indirect address. (Digital Equipment calls its form of indirect addressing "deferred" addressing.)

The four basic address modes are as follows:

Register: Contains the operand.

Auto-increment: Register content is the operand address; then register content is incremented.

Auto-decrement: Register content is decremented and then used as the operand address.

Index: Content of the memory location following the instructions word plus the content of the selected register is used as the operand address.

The following four additional modes are generated if the indirect bit is set.

Register deferred (indirect): Register contains the address of the operand.

Autoincrement deferred (indirect): Register content is used as the address of the operand address; then content is incremented.

Autodecrement deferred (indirect): Register content is decremented and then used as the address of the operand address.

Index deferred (indirect): Content of the memory location following the instruction word plus the content of the selected register is used as the address of the operand address.

Stack Addressing   Stack processing facilities are inherent in the auto-increment and auto-decrement addressing modes. A stack is a buffer used for the temporary storage of data. A pushdown stack has the special characteristics that the last item (unit of data) put on the stack is the first item read out of the stack. A stack is implemented by dedicating a block of memory locations to it, such as locations 100 to 199.

A register can be used to store the stack pointer. The auto-decrement addressing mode is used to put items on a stack (PDP-11 stacks are built downward in memory), and the autoincrement mode is used to pop items from a stack. If the items stored on the stack are operand address, the autoincrement and autodecrement deferred modes are used to push and pop the stack.

A pushdown stack can be built upward or downward in memory. If built upward, the first item put on the stack is stored in location 100 (for our example), the next in 101, and so on. The last item is stored in location 199 and the stack is full. If built downward, the first item is put in location 199, the second in location 198, and so on. When the last item is put in location 100, the stack is full.

In computer jargon, an item is "pushed onto" (stored on) a stack or "popped" (read and removed) from a stack. When all items have been popped from the stack, it is empty. A stack pointer always addresses the next item to be popped from the stack. It is incremented (decremented if the stack is built downward in memory) before it is used as the address for pushing an item onto the stack; it is decremented (incremented if the stack is built downward in memory) after an item is popped from the stack.

Stack-processing facilities make it possible to develop efficient assemblers, compilers, I/O routines, interrupt service routines, subroutines, operating systems, and user programs. Pushdown stacks have inherent nesting capability, which make them efficient for storing processor status when switching between the main program and service routines for I/O devices and interrupts or subroutines. They are also useful for passing parameters between main programs and subroutines, which are commonly reentrant. (A reentrant subroutine can be called by a high priority program while it is executing for a lower priority program.)

If the program counter, which is one of the general-purpose registers on the PDP-11, is selected as the register in the auto-increment mode, the word in the location following the instruction word is addressed. Thus, the instruction is effectively two words long, and the second word stores the operand for immediate addressing. If the program counter is selected as the register in the indexed addressing mode, the address calculation is the same as for relative addressing.

The indexed mode treats the word following the instruction word as a base address, which is indexed by the content of the selected register. This mode is the same as indexed addressing on other computers, except that both the displacement and the indexer are full words.

The PDP-11 addresses to the byte level, so its 16-bit word can address 65,578 bytes or 32,768 words. Maximum memory size for the PDP-11/40 and 11/45 is 126,968 words. (Just in case you believe a number that is not a power of 2 is a mistake in a book on computers, the PDP-11/40 and 11/45 have addresses for 131,072 words of memory, but the upper 6K addresses are used for other purposes.) The problem of addressing more memory locations than there are possible number combinations in the computer word has been around longer than the PDP-11, but it has been solved in various ways.

Bank and Virtual Memory Addressing   Minicomputer manufacturers have usually solved the problem by grouping blocks of memory locations together. These blocks are usually called "banks." The number of memory locations within a bank cannot exceed the addressing capability of the computer word: 4K words for a 12-bit machine, 32K words for a 16-bit machine, and so on. A program can address only those memory locations within the bank that contains the program. A separate small register, one or two bits long, specifies the bank address for physical memory. Special instructions are included in the instruction set to load the bank address register for switching from one memory bank to another.

The PDP-11/40 and 11/45 do not use bank addressing; they use a memory management system that also implements virtual addressing. In virtual addressing, the addresses calculated by the program are virtual addresses and are sent to a memory management system, which translates them into physical memory addresses. Sending a 16-bit virtual address through a translator can relocate addresses in physical memory but it produces only a 16-bit physical address, which can still address only 32K words of memory. The memory management system must find more address bits. The PDP-11/40 and 11/45 obtain one bit from the processor mode and another bit from the memory access mode, whether it is for an instruction or for data (an operand). (The 11/40 has two processor modes and the 11/45 has three; so, the 11/45 actually obtains 1.5 addressing bits. See PDP-11 Report in the Appendix A.) Because large memories were planned for in the original PDP-11 design, the data paths between units in a PDP-11 system are 18-bits wide to allow the transfer of 18-bit addresses or data.

The processor mode and access mode combined with the three most significant bits of the address word select an active page register, which contains a page address field. A page is a group of contiguous memory locations treated as a storage unit. The page address field is combined with the 13 least significant bits of the calculated address to produce an 18-bit physical memory address.

Virtual-memory addressing via a memory management system allows sophisticated operating systems to utilize memory space efficiently, particularly in multiprogramming environments where many different programs can be in main memory concurrently. Some programs are long; some are short. The memory space vacated by a program that is finished may not be large enough for the next program scheduled for execution. Memory, however, may have other empty spaces so that the large program could be loaded if all the empty space were treated as one contiguous block of locations in memory. Virtual addressing allows the operating system to do this by loading the registers in the memory management system with the appropriate physical addresses. To make housekeeping (processor time devoted to executing instructions that maintain order in the system) less of a burden, memory management systems limit the size of the memory blocks that can be handled. In the case of the PDP-11, block size can range from 32 to 4096 words in increments of 32 words.

Most minicomputers do not have virtual-memory addressing. Prior to the introduction of the PDP-11/40 and 11/45, only the Systems Engineering SEL 72 had it, but in a different form. It has been implemented on a number of large-scale computers for several years, and the concept has been revived as an active topic for discussion since IBM announced it for the System/370. The difficulty with virtual-memory addressing is the complexity of the operating system needed to control it. An operating system for it was scheduled for release in 1973.

Interrupt Systems

An interrupt is a signal that causes the processor to suspend the execution of instructions in the current program and to branch to a set of instructions that deal with the interrupt condition. When the interrupt has been taken care of, the processor continues to execute the suspended program.

The interrupt system makes the computer responsive to the outside world. It also allows the computer to diagnose and handle error and alarm conditions and other events that are asynchronous to its efficient operation. Interrupts can be classified as external interrupts and internal interrupts; internal interrupts are sometimes called "traps." External interrupts are those associated with devices that are external to the processor.

Peripheral devices and human operators do not function at the same speed as the processor; furthermore, they usually function at an unpredictable or imprecise rate of speed. An operator, for example, may type 50 words per minute on the average, but the time between key strokes will vary considerably, depending on the location of the key and other factors. The processor operates at high speed and can store in a few microseconds the character an operator types. The processor would spend most of its time waiting if it devoted its time exclusively to inputting the characters an operator is typing. So, the processor performs other functions and devotes itself to inputting a character only after an interrupt signals that the character has been typed and is waiting to be transferred. Once the character has been transferred, the processor returns to the program it was executing when the interrupt occurred. The program that was executed to transfer the character from the keyboard to the processor's main memory is the interrupt servicing routine for the keyboard.

All peripheral devices communicate with the processor in similar fashion via the interrupt system. A computer system can include many peripherals that perform different functions. The processor must service each one upon demand. To do this, a service routine is stored in main memory for each peripheral device. The interrupt system determines which device requires service and selects the appropriate service routine for execution. The service routines for peripheral devices are called I/O handlers, and the group of service routines for all the peripheral devices in the system is commonly called the input/output programming system (IOPS).

External Interrupts   Interrupt systems are implemented by a combination of hardware and software. Generally, a peripheral device can have a number of conditions that can cause an interrupt, but only one hardware interrupt is allotted to the device. The I/O handler examines a status word that is associated with the device to determine the cause of the interrupt: error, malfunction, character ready for transfer, operation finished, end of block, or some conditions peculiar to the device. Because the handler is written specifically for the device, all its characteristics and service needs can be taken into account.

The simplest interrupt system has a single interrupt line and a single interrupt level. All devices send signals over the same line at the same level. The interrupt servicing software establishes a priority interrupt structure by the order in which it tests the interrupt status of devices. The highest priority device is tested first, the next highest priority device second, and so on, with the lowest priority device last.

A somewhat more complex interrupt system is a single line, multilevel system. Priority level is established by the order in which devices are connected to the interrupt line. The line is connected to devices in a daisy-chain fashion so that the first device on the line has highest priority, the second device has the next highest priority, down to the last device, which has lowest priority. When the processor accepts an interrupt, which is usually between instructions, the first device with an interrupt pending on the line responds by sending its device address or interrupt vector (address of device service routine) to the processor. The processor uses the address or interrupt vector to select the interrupt service routine of the device.

More complex interrupt systems are multiline and multilevel. Each line has a fixed priority with respect to the other lines. In addition, multiple devices can be connected to each line; the order in which these devices are connected to lines further establishes device priority, as described above.

Generally, a minicomputer processor can support as many external interrupts as the number of devices it can address. The number ranges from 16 on some systems to 256 or more on others. The limiting factor is usually the time required for the software routines to service the devices and is not associated with interrupt hardware.

Internal Interrupts   The internal interrupt system, or trap system, provides for generating signals that identify abnormal or occasional conditions within the system, such as the following:

Illegal instruction code.

Illegal address.

Memory protection violation.

Memory parity error.

Trap instruction (for debugging).

Bus error (too much time elapsed between signals).

Watchdog timer not reset.

Interval timer reached setting.

Overflow from fixed-point arithmetic operation (number too large, division by zero).

Overflow or underflow for floating-point operation (exponent too large or too small).

Switch on control panel set.

Power failure.

Power restart.

Every system does not implement all these trap conditions, but most implement those associated with the hardware in the system. Most do trap instruction codes not applicable to the system. Some do not trap illegal addresses but use a wrap-around addressing scheme. For example, if a system has only 8K words of memory and an address beyond 8192 is generated, the processor uses the address module 8192. Thus, an address of 12,044 is handled the same as an address of 3852 (12,044 − 8192 = 3852).

A number of minicomputer systems do not implement memory parity or memory protect even as options. Most systems provide some means for establishing breakpoints in a program, either through a switch on the control panel or by setting a trace bit in the processor status word. The switch or the trace bit is reset when the program is executed and set only for program debugging.

Some systems have a bus-error detection circuit or a watchdog timer to signal the operator is the system is not running at the proper speed or is halted. If too much time elapses between certain events, such as between synchronization signals on the I/O bus or between memory accesses, the interrupt system signals an alarm (a buzzer or bell).

Many systems have timers as standard equipment or as options to use for calculating the time of day and elapsed time between events. The timers are programmable and can be used to schedule programs for execution and to monitor events. The interrupt system signals the processor when a particular amount of time has elapsed. The service routine can increment counters that will calculate time of day and the timed intervals needed by the application.

Overflow or underflow interrupts allow the program to recover from errors made because the data is out of bounds.

Some systems use switches on the control panel as a means for the operator to communicate with the system directly. The switch generates an interrupt that can initiate different programs depending on its setting. Other systems use a switch for an operator interrupt; the operator can then type in systems control parameters when the interrupt is granted.

When power fails, all systems provide some means to delay shutdown for a few milliseconds, to allow preparation for restarting. A power-fail interrupt service routine can transfer the contents of internal registers to memory before shutdown. Core memory does not lose its content when power is removed. Semiconductor memory does lose its content when power is removed, but most systems that use semiconductor memory have a standby battery for temporary memory power during a power failure.

The power-restart interrupt signals the service routine to reload the internal registers from memory to continue program execution.

MEMORY

The internal memory may be composed of read/write core or solid state semiconductor memory modules, or, for some small control systems, a read-only memory. Core memory is the most common type of memory used, although semiconductor memories are gaining in popularity. To date, only Texas Instruments' TI 960A and TI 980A use semiconductor memories exclusively. Small read-only memories are available for many systems.

Systems that operate like hardwired controllers may use only read-only memory. Many systems allow a combination of core, semiconductor, and read-only memories.

Core Memory

Core memory has a number of advantages. It has been in use for about 12 years; it is readily available, has become very reliable, and is relatively inexpensive. It is quite fast, with cycle times ranging from 0.650 to 1.2 ms for a 16-bit word. Modules range in size from 1024 to 8192 words. Core memory retains its content indefinitely when power is removed. For all these reasons, core is still the most popular type of internal memory.

Semiconductor Memory

Semiconductor memory is faster than core memory with cycle times ranging from 150 to 400 ns (= 1×10^{-9} sec) for a 16-bit word. It is currently more expensive than core memory, but this should change as more semiconductor houses produce memories in large quantities and refine their production techniques. Semiconductor memory loses its content when power is removed, thus standby power, usually a battery, must be supplied. As a practical matter, standby power must also be supplied for core memory systems if system shutdown cannot be tolerated. Semiconductor memory modules are available in 256 to 8192 words, but most minicomputer manufacturers supply only small modules of 1024, 2048, or 4096 words for their systems. The small memories are used for scratchpad memory (like a note pad for intermediate calculations) or for storing frequently used subroutines. Most control memories in microprogrammed processors use semiconductor memory modules because of their speed.

Read-only Memory

Read-only memories are more commonly used for bootstrap (start from zero memory) loaders for paper tape, magnetic tape, disk, or any other input device. They are sometimes used to store and protect real-time programs that are run with user programs in a multiprogramming environment.

Memory Characteristics

Most core memory modules operate asynchronously with respect to the processor. A memory cycle begins when the processor requires access to memory. During the first half of the cycle, the information is read out of memory. Because read-out destroys the memory content, the last half of the cycle is used to write the content back into memory. The processor can begin using the data as soon as it is read out, so the processor's operation overlaps the write half-cycle when instructions or operands are read from memory. Because of this read/write characteristic of core memory, memory modules are often grouped together in pairs; even addresses are assigned to one module and odd addresses to the other module. This is called "interleaving," and it increases the probability that a memory READ from one module will overlap the memory WRITE to the other module.

Most systems have only one memory bus and one memory port (entry). Peripheral devices and the processor must share the bus. If a peripheral requires memory access to transfer a word in or out of memory at the same time the processor requires access, common practice is to give the peripheral device priority. This is called "cycle stealing"; the peripheral device steals memory cycles as needed from the processor to transfer data.

Some systems have two or more ports to memory: one is used by the processor and the other(s) can be used by high-speed peripheral devices or by another processor. Multiple ports are most common for systems used for high speed data acquisition systems or for multiprocessor systems. In these cases, a second port can almost double system throughput (total amount of useful work done).

Memory word length varies from 8 to 24 bits. Memory parity adds one bit per byte or word. The parity bit is generated and stored each time a word is written into memory; it is recalculated and checked for each word read out of memory. Memory parity can be odd or even. It is usually odd, so that a word of zeros has at least one bit in it.

Memory Protect

Memory protect provides a means of protecting certain areas of memory so that programs stored there cannot be inadvertently destroyed. Memory protect is essential for multiprogramming environments where different programs are in memory concurrently and are executing at different times. For example, in real-time systems with foreground/background processing, the real-time system executes in the foreground and must be protected from a background program being debugged.

Some systems provide a fence register, which marks the boundary between protected and unprotected memory. Programs executing from unprotected memory cannot write in any location in protected memory or cannot access any location in protected memory for any reason whatsoever. Unprotected programs can communicate with protected programs only through the interrupt system or the operating system. Programs executing from protected memory can access any location in memory.

Other systems provide upper and lower limit registers that confine a program to its allotted area of core. In this case, the operating system assigns memory to each program as it is loaded into memory. Compilers and assemblers that produce relocatable output code are designed to make relocation of programs possible by calculating all addresses as relative to the program counter or a base register.

A set of privileged instructions is associated with memory protection; these instructions can be executed only by programs executing from protected memory. These include I/O instructions, halt, and control instructions that change control registers or processor status.

INPUT/OUTPUT CONTROL

Data is transferred between a peripheral device and the processor by two main methods: programmed I/O (PIO) or Direct Memory Access (DMA). The latter is comparable to a selector channel on large computers. Some systems also have a variation on DMA that is comparable to a multiplexer channel in large computers.

Programmed I/O

All minicomputers have a PIO facility. An I/O instruction transfers one word between a peripheral device and a processor internal register or a main memory location. The word can be a control, data, or status word, depending on the device and the instruction. An I/O instruction combined with a control word can turn a device on or off, start a card through a reader or a tape moving, rewind a tape, get a device ready for operation, or test certain device conditions. Input/output instructions are device-dependent, and bits in the control word are interpreted according to the peculiarities of the device. Each device has a number of flags (flip-flops that store status bits until they are used) associated with it. Instructions are usually provided to test some of the flags individually and to transfer all flags to the processor in a status word, which the program can examine. Flags signal such conditions as device ready, device malfunction, interrupt pending, end-of-tape, end of block, error detected, and other conditions appropriate for the device.

Programmed I/O instructions also transfer data for slow-speed devices and load parameters for block transfers by high-speed devices that use the DMA facility. Several instructions are usually needed to prepare the device and/or the channel for DMA transfers. High-speed devices, such as magnetic tape and disk drives, transfer blocks of data directly to or from memory under control of the DMA facility.

Direct Memory Access

Some systems implement DMA as a channel that controls the transfer. Control registers, a word count register, and a current address register are located in the channel. The channel steals a memory cycle to transfer a word, increments the current address, and decrements the word count. When the word count reaches zero, the channel signals an end-of-block interrupt. Although a number of devices can connect to the DMA channel, only one device at a time can use the channel because it has only one set of control registers. Additional DMA channels must be added to the system іі more than one device is to transfer data simultaneously.

A few systems chain block transfers by using a group of control words stored in main memory to set up the parameters for each block transfer. In this case, the PIO instruction transfers the address of the first control word in memory. The DMA channel then loads the current address and word-count registers from memory. When the block transfer is completed and chaining is specified, the channel loads the channel registers with the next group of control words in memory. This continues until all blocks have been transferred; the last group of control words does not specify chaining, and the channel signals an interrupt.

Other systems implement DMA as a channel that can access memory directly, but it contains no control registers. Each controller for the high-speed devices that transfer data over DMA must have its own set of control registers and its own control logic for incrementing the current address and decrementing the word count. For these systems, any number of high-speed devices can transfer data concurrently by timesharing the DMA channel. The aggregate data rate of all devices transferring data simultaneously, however, cannot exceed the rate allowed by the memory cycle rate.

Multiplexer Channels

If a multiplexer channel is implemented, it contains control registers that are shared by all the devices using the channel. The control words for each device are stored in dedicated locations in main memory. Each time a device transfers a word, its current address and word count are loaded into the channel registers, the word is transferred, and then the control registers are updated and stored back in the dedicated locations in memory. This procedure requires five memory accesses—two to load the control registers, one to transfer the data word, and two to store the control registers back in main memory; thus, the maximum data transfer rate is one-fifth that of a DMA channel. Some multiplexer channels do skip the operation that loads the control registers if a device uses the channel for successive transfers without any intervening transfers by other devices. This can be done because the control registers contain the current address and word count from the previous transfer.

Data Transfer Rates

The maximum data transfer rate using PIO transfers depends on the device-software servicing routines, but it usually is about 50,000 words per second. Maximum data transfer rate via DMA is a direct function of the memory cycle time, one million words per second for a 1 µs (microsecond) memory cycle rate. Maximum transfer rate via a multiplexer channel is from one-third to one-fifth that of DMA, depending on the number of devices using the channel simultaneously.

Because PIO transfers halt processing and DMA and multiplexer channels steal memory cycles from the processor for data transfers, a system can be overloaded by peripheral devices and spend all its time on I/O operations. Some minicomputers in computer networks are dedicated to peripheral processing or to servicing data communication lines.

For systems that are designed for heavy processing loads and high I/O transfer rates, the memory modules often have two entry ports, one for the processor and one for peripheral devices. With multiple memory ports, cycle stealing for DMA transfers halts the processor only if the processor and the DMA channel try to access the same module simultaneously. Good system planning will reduce the number of conflicts for memory access, and multiple ports can almost double the system throughput. Other structures can also be arranged. For example, the PDP-11/45 has a memory bus that connects high-speed semiconductor memory modules to the processor and another bus that connects the processor to the core memory and to peripheral devices. A program can execute programs from semiconductor memory and devices can transfer data to or from core memory without any interference between the two. In practice, the processor must periodically transfer data between core memory and semiconductor memory in order to use the data that is input and to generate data for output, and therefore some conflicts for core memory access will arise.

Interleaving memory modules, as mentioned in the Memory Section, allows overlapping the read half cycle from one module with the write half cycle of another module. This also can increase system throughput substantially.

SUMMARY

Although minicomputers are designed as general-purpose systems, their mainframes vary markedly for a number of reasons, such as:

Compatibility with older systems that have strong software support.

New technology that makes alternative designs feasible, such as high-speed control memories that make microprogrammed processors competive with hard-wired processors.

Marketing strategies of the manufacturer; that is, the mainframe is oriented toward a specific market.

Compromises required to optimize flexibility, processing power, and cost.

As this list indicates, sheer processing capability is only one factor in determining minicomputer design. System considerations are more important. As the minicomputer industry has grown and prospered, a large customer base of experienced users has been built up. These users are far more concerned with total system integration into their business than they are with sheer processing power.

3. MINICOMPUTER PERIPHERALS DEVICES

The importance of minicomputer peripherals is demonstrated by the fact that over 60 percent of the price of an average system is for peripheral equipment. In the past few years, minicomputer peripherals have declined in price while the number and types have increased. Although peripherals are usually purchased along with the mainframe from the mainframe manufacturer, few minicomputer manufacturers make their own peripherals. Most manufacturers buy them from an independent OEM supplier, add their own control electronics, develop software support, and provide maintenance service in the package offered to the minicomputer user.

Interestingly, the cost of the control electronics can approach that of the device itself. Typical ranges for the percentage of total peripheral cost represented by the controller, in minimum-capacity disk and tape systems, are 35 to 40 percent and 30 to 35 percent, respectively. Furthermore, the extensive additions made by the mainframe manufacturer to the peripherals can result in profits running as high as those on the mainframe itself. Control electronics costs, however, should benefit from the improving price/performance of semiconductor circuits and may well yield price reductions in minicomputer peripherals.

The OEM peripherals market is a very competitive one, and minicomputer mainframe manufacturers frequently change their suppliers as first one and then another appears to offer advantages in price, performance, or reliability. This readiness to change suppliers means that minicomputers introduced by different manufacturers at about the same time tend to have peripherals with similar specifications. There is some variation in

46

price, however, due to different marketing approaches.

Minicomputer peripherals are divided into four major categories:

1. Conventional slow-speed input/output devices: console typewriter, paper tape readers and punches, card readers and punches, and serial line printers (Fig. 3-1).

2. Mass storage input/output devices: cassette tapes (Fig. 3-2), small non-industry-standard magnetic tape units, industry-standard magnetic tape drives, fixed-head disk or drum drives, and movable-head disk-pack or disk cartridge drives.

3. Special-purpose devices: displays (Fig. 3-3), plotters, analog-to-digital (A/D) and digital-to-analog (D/A) converters and subsystems, and digital interfaces.

4. Data communication interfaces and terminals (Fig. 3-4): single line interfaces to standard communication lines, subsystems or multiplexers for servicing multiple lines, Teletype or other keyboard terminals, and display terminals.

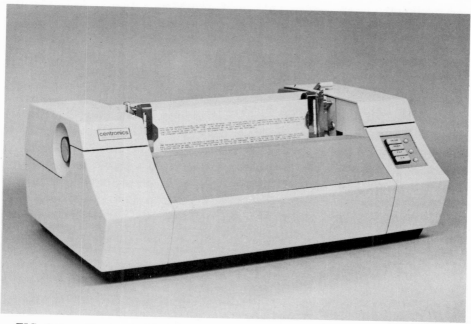

FIG. 3-1.   Centronics Model 101 printer—Prints 165 characters per second on standard paper, original and four copies.

FIG. 3-2.   TU60 DEC cassette produced by Digital Equipment Corporation for its PDP-8 and PDP-11 computers.

Every minicomputer system does not support all of these devices, although most systems support some devices in each category. Systems oriented toward a particular market will provide many devices peculiar to that market. For example, a system extensively marketed for data communications will have many more data communications interfaces than a system marketed extensively for process control. The system oriented toward process control will have many A/D and D/A converters and sub-systems and digital interfaces.

Most systems support an assortment of slow-speed peripherals to provide communication with the operator and the outside world, one or more mass storage devices for the storage of programs and data, and a number of data communication and special-purpose devices for the system's major application area. Large manufacturers, such as Digital Equipment, Data General, Hewlett-Packard, Varian Data Machines, and Honeywell, market their systems across the board and provide a large assortment of peripheral

FIG. 3-3.   Data General Corporation Nova Display 6010, designed as a low-cost, high-speed visual display terminal.

devices in all categories. They will provide a number of models for each device type to provide a range of performance characteristics and price. For example, several models of line printers will be offered with different size character sets, line widths, and printing speeds.

SLOW-SPEED PERIPHERALS

Slow-speed devices provide communication between the operator and/or the outside world and the computer. The minimum needed is a keyboard for input and a visual record and a printer for visual output. The cheapest device for these operations is a Teletype KSR 33, which separates the keyboard input function from the printer output function. The printer operates at 10 characters per second.

To automate the system somewhat and to allow computer output from one operation to be used for computer input to another, a paper tape

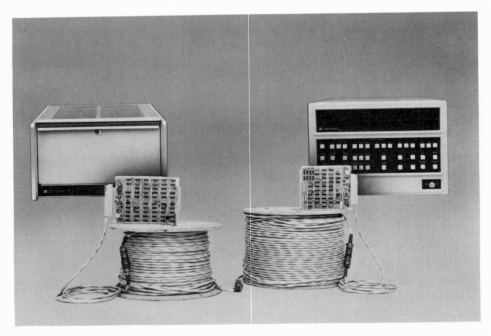

FIG. 3-4.   With high-speed Serial Data Communication capability, remote terminals like the HP-2570A coupler/controller (left) or HP-2100A computer (right)
the system has two-way communication over a four-wire cable with a central
2100A computer.

reader and punch is usually added. The Teletype ASR 33 conveniently
combines a keyboard, printer, and paper tape reader/punch into one inexpensive unit, which operates at 10 characters per second for the printer
and the paper tape reader and punch. A Teletype ASR 33 is available for all
minicomputers except those manufactured by IBM: System 7, 1130, and
1800. For systems with only an ASR 33, the paper tape stores programs
and data. Source programs can be input from the paper tape reader, assembled or compiled and output to the paper tape punch for future use.
The object code can be read from the paper tape reader for debugging or
for execution.

    This small system is complete for program development and execution,
but it is not very fast. It can be upgraded by using a Teletype KSR 33 for
keyboard and printer and adding a high-speed paper tape reader and punch.
The reader speed is usually around 300 characters per second and the
punch speed around 50 or 65 characters per second.

    If the KSR 33 printer is too slow for the visual records required, a separate and faster printer can be added, a serial printer that operates at 30 to 165 characters per second or a line printer that operates from 200 to over 1000 lines per minute. The newer electrostatic printers are fast and inexpensive. The older impact line printers are still in business, offering a full range of character set sizes, line widths, and speed.

Card readers are commonly used as an input device in place of or in addition to a paper tape reader. This is particularly true when the minicomputer is part of a larger computer system and key punches are readily available for card preparation. Cards are more commonly used than paper tape for large computers.

Although card readers are relatively inexpensive, card punches are very expensive and rarely available as a minicomputer output device. Generally, they are available only for applications where the minicomputer output is used as input by large computers. Even here, industry standard magnetic tape is a more common medium of exchange between computers and is no more expensive than a card punch.

Punched cards have one prime advantage over paper tape; they are unit records. A card can be taken out and thrown away off line (not connected to the computer, as opposed to on-line or connection to the computer) and a new card inserted. Tapes are serial devices, and they are not easy to correct. Corrections require that the tape be duplicated up to the record to be changed, the new data inserted, and the rest of the tape duplicated. If done on line, the computer is tied up while the tape is being corrected. Tape duplicating is not a highly efficient use of a computer.

Depending on the system use, another kind of device can be used for the Teletype KSR 33, perhaps a keyboard with a small display.

MASS STORAGE DEVICES

Because of the limited size of internal computer memory, mass storage devices have been developed to operate as an extension of computer memory. These range from a magnetic tape cassette that can store about 200,000 bytes, to a large disk pack drive that can store up to 20 million bytes.

The tape cassettes and nonindustry-standard magnetic tape devices automate a system in a way unavailable to paper tape systems. Punched paper tape output must be manually loaded into a paper tape reader for input. Magnetic tapes can be rewound under program control so that tape output can be used as input without any human intervention. For small systems, the addition of even one tape cassette is a major system upgrade because it allows an entirely different kind of system operation. Programs can be stored on the tape and the appropriate program selected for execution as new jobs or new job parameters are called for from the keyboard or the paper tape reader. The system operation can be changed rapidly by loading a new cassette.

The primary nonindustry-standard magnetic tape available for minicomputers is Digital Equipment's DEC tape, which was one of the earliest, inexpensive mass storage devices available for minicomputers. It is available only for Digital's own minicomputers, but the company produces about 40 percent of all minicomputers sold and the use of DEC tape is widespread.

DEC tape is unique in that it is block-addressable, and can be read either forward or backward. Maximum storage capacity is about 275,000 bytes. Users become addicted to DEC tape because it is very reliable and the reels are small (3½ inches in diameter) and lightweight so that they can be carried around in a pocketbook or pocket. In addition, Digital provides extensive software for systems that use only DEC tape for mass storage. The tape performs the same system functions for Digital's PDP (Programmed Data Processor) computers as those performed by cassette tapes for other systems.

Industry-standard magnetic tape drives with seven and nine tracks are common media of exchange between computers. A tape reel can store about 10 million bytes, and is small enough to be carried from one location to another. Also, since magnetic tapes have been used with computers for over 20 years, they are readily available and have been proved reliable. Many techniques have been developed to use them for different kinds of data processing. Because magnetic tape is a serial device, it is an efficient storage medium for data that is used in a serial fashion. However, it is inefficient for storing data that is used in a random fashion, because tapes must be moved back and forth to locate data. Although tapes are relatively fast, moving up to 150 inches per second, they are slow in relationship to internal processing speed, which is measured in microseconds (ms) or even nanoseconds (ns). Another disadvantage is that insertion of data requires that the tape be duplicated.

Since disk storage has become readily available and inexpensive, magnetic tapes are used more for backup storage and as a medium of exchange rather than for active mass storage. Magnetic tapes are considerably cheaper than disk in terms of cost per byte stored.

Disk storage drives are called "random access" devices, although they are a combination of random-serial access devices. Data is stored in tracks on a flat, circular disk surface. Fixed or moving read/write heads select the track, but once a track is selected, the data is read or written in a serial fashion. Fixed-head disks can select a track quickly because each track has its own dedicated read/write head and selection involves only electronic circuits. Moving-head disks are slow at track selection because one read/

write head is used to read or record all tracks on a disk surface and must move to the track before reading or recording can begin. Once the track is selected, however, fixed- and moving-head disks read or record data at the same rate of speed.

Moving-head disks are generally disk packs or disk cartridges in which 2 to 20 disk surfaces are combined into one unit; cartridges have 2 or 4 surfaces and disk packs have 10 or 20. An arm assembly with one read/write per surface in the disk pack or cartridge moves as a unit when a track is selected. Thus, from each arm position, one track of data can be read from each disk surface; this amount of data is called a "cylinder."

Fixed-head disks are considerably more expensive (about 10 cents per byte) than moving-head disks per byte of storage (about 0.3 cents per byte). To gain most efficient use of mass storage devices, most systems use fixed-head disks to store intermediate data and programs that are frequently swapped in and out of main memory. Moving-head disks, particularly disk packs, are used to store master or relatively stable data that is accessed mostly in a serial fashion so that head movement is kept to a minimum, usually track-to-track. Disk cartridges, which are between fixed-head disks and disk packs in storage capacity, speed, and cost per byte of storage, are frequently used to store programs, intermediate data, and master data.

The whole problem associated with the use of mass storage devices and their management is a specialized field of study. How data is organized in the master file (the data base), how it is accessed, how records are added to or deleted from the file affect system efficiency. Further, the records—which are frequently 5, 10, 15, or more words long—are application-oriented and therefore the way in which items are organized within records is important.

SPECIAL-PURPOSE I/O DEVICES

Although special-purpose I/O devices are application-oriented, most are useful for many different kinds of jobs. Displays and plotters, for example, are graphic devices and are used to condense and present data in the terms commonly used by architects, doctors, engineers, stock brokers, mathematicians, and other professionals. Standard-sized plotters are available for a number of minicomputers. They are used to output data in a graphical form. The large flat-bed plotters designed to draw plans for a large shopping center, for example, are not peripheral to a minicomputer. In this case, it is the other way around; the minicomputer is used as a control unit for the plotting system (Fig. 3-5).

Displays can also present graphical data, but they do not provide a hard copy. For this purpose a printer is often available as an optional feature.

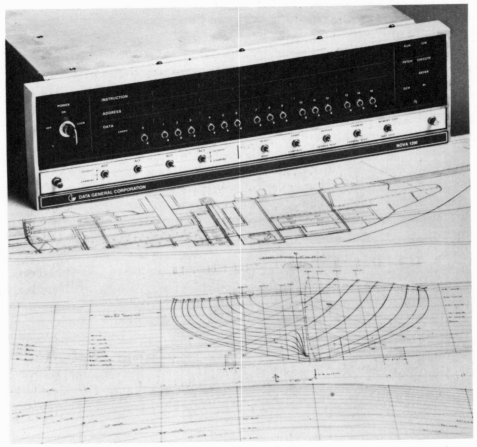

FIG. 3-5.   Data General Corporation Nova 1200 computer lets racing boat designers test effects of design changes via computerized model of the boat.

Usually a character generator is also optionally available so that text can be displayed. Displays are popular I/O devices because they can be interactive; that is, an operator can change the text or the graph and check it visually before it is read into the computer. Graphs are changed by the operator's tracing in the data with a lightpen. Text is changed via a keyboard, which is also an optional feature.

Interactive displays have many uses. They are used as terminals for billing and inventory control; computer-aided instruction; laboratory work; design, test, and measurement; and many other applications. They are useful for commercial data-entry systems because information can be entered from a keyboard and checked on the display. If any character is in error, it can be corrected and the complete item displayed before any characters are stored in the computer's memory (Fig. 3-6).

FIG. 3-6. Centronics Data Computer Model 401 CRT keyboard display terminal.

Other special-purpose devices, such as A/D and D/A converters and digital interfaces, connect noncomputer devices to the minicomputer system. Many measuring and control devices generate or use analog data; the minicomputer operates on digital data only. Converters are necessary to change analog data to digital data on input and to change it back on output. When a number of analog devices are used with the minicomputer, multiplexers connect groups of devices to one A/D converter input. For output, modules that connect two, four, or more devices are sometimes available. Special configurations of A/D and D/A converters are often available to address and control 8, 16, 32, 64, or more lines from special-purpose devices.

Digital interfaces transfer a word of data between a device and the computer. Sometimes the word is treated as two half-words or as 16 individual bits, with each bit performing a control function on output or reading a status function on input.

DATA COMMUNICATIONS

With the increasing use of computer networks, minicomputers are operating as data concentrators, preprocessors, message switchers, and remote terminals. Most "intelligent" or "smart" terminals become intelligent or smart by incorporating a minicomputer. Intelligent terminals do some processing as well as operating as a remote input or output device. They communicate with other computers and terminals over communication lines, primarily by voice grade or broad band telephone lines, and sometimes by telegraph lines. The Federal Communications Commission specifies the standards that must be maintained on communication lines and the devices that can connect to them. Minicomputer manufacturers provide interfaces to standard devices connected to communication lines so that data can be input and output to and from them.

Although data communication networks have been operating successfully for four or five years, the industry is in its infancy and very unsophisticated. Networks are painstakingly built, and it is only the sheer processing capability of computers that makes them work at all.

When operating as a data concentrator, the minicomputer inputs data character from a number of low-speed communication lines, checks it, assembles it into messages, and transmits it at high speed to a central computer for processing.

Terminals

The word "terminal" is used broadly and can mean anything from a keyboard to a complete processing system with data communication facilities. Terminals for minicomputers are simply remote devices for inputting and outputting data into and out of the computer. They are generally confined to interactive keyboard and display devices.

SUMMARY

Peripherals represent a significant part of the minicomputer system, not only in terms of system cost but also system performance. Large manufacturers offer a broad range of peripherals so that a system can be configured to meet the needs of a specific application. Most minicomputer manufacturers do not make their own peripherals but buy them OEM and develop the interface and control. Thus, it is no accident that many peripherals from different manufacturers have similar performance characteristics. The minicomputer market has become so large that peripheral manufacturers are scaling their products to the needs of the minicomputer user. Peripherals are still expensive in relation to the basic cost of the processor and memory. This is due primarily to the dramatic drop in processor and memory costs in the past few years and not to inactivity in the peripherals area. Peripheral prices have also dropped, but not quite so dramatically.

4. MINICOMPUTER SOFTWARE

Software, once suffering from benign neglect by the minicomputer manufacturers, is as important as the hardware to a minicomputer system. Digital Equipment, for example, devotes as much staff time to software development as to hardware development. Because most minicomputer manufacturers started as OEM suppliers, a minimal amount of software was developed—an assembler, utilities for loading and debugging, mathematical subroutines, and perhaps a FORTRAN compiler. As manufacturers began to address the end-user market, more software was required, but the end-users of the first minicomputers were relatively sophisticated and developed much of their own software.

To sustain the continued growth of the minicomputer market, once the most eager and more knowledgeable customers were satisfied, new markets had to be developed. Systems became larger and required more extensive operating systems. New users were less sophisticated and demanded more system support, higher-level languages, operating systems, and application packages. Today, no serious minicomputer manufacturer can be competitive without a substantial investment in system software.

The kind of software required will vary according to the primary market addressed, but for across-the-board competition the following functional modules must be included:

1. Software to support a small stand-alone system operating as a desk calculator—uses a higher-level language such as BASIC or FOCAL for single and multiple users.

58

2. Modular operating system for program development and execution (batch operating system)—handles all I/O and interrupts; communicates with the operator; loads, assembles, or compiles, and executes programs; provides source-code editing facilities; manages files.

3. Assemblers for both absolute and relocatable code.

4. Compilers for higher-level languages such as FORTRAN, ALGOL, RPG (Report Program Generator), or COBOL-like language.

5. Modular real-time operating system for running real-time programs concurrently with background program development and execution—schedules all jobs and executes them on a priority basis; executes background jobs in free time; communicates with operator; handles all I/O and interrupts; manages files.

6. Programs for several specific applications.

7. Utilities for debugging, hardware diagnosis, loading, dumps, and editing.

8. Subroutines library for fixed-point arithmetic (multiply, divide, double precision), floating-point arithmetic, conversion between data formats (decimal and binary, fixed point and floating point), and trigometric functions.

Although manufacturers vary in the amount of software they supply free with a system, most manufacturers charge for unusual, elaborate, or application-oriented software. This allows them to sell small systems with simple software at very low costs because the price does not include a pro-rated share of the expensive software development costs. Most manufacturers supply without charge a collection of programs or even an operating system for program development, assembler, BASIC or FOCAL interpreters, utilities, and subroutine library. Practically all charge for a real-time operating system, a higher-level language compiler (FORTRAN IV, ALGOL, RPG, or COBOL-like language), and applications packages. Sometimes, almost all system software that can run on the user's configuration is supplied free, particularly if the older system is one for which software was developed over a number of years.

OPERATING SYSTEMS

All systems have software to support program development and execution. For small systems with only a Teletype ASR 33 for I/O, software may consist of little more than I/O handlers, interrupt servicing routines, an assembler, and perhaps a FORTRAN compiler, utilities and a subroutine library.

System control resides in the operator who loads the system with the appropriate programs and sequences for their execution.

The collection of programs used for this kind of system cannot be classified as an operating system because it does not provide centralized software control. A complete operating system performs all functions required for programmed system control. It communicates with the operator to request parameters or to report status, loads, links, and sequence programs for execution, assigns I/O devices to programs, performs all I/O operations, and services interrupts. Generally, a full-fledged operating system requires a mass-storage device to store programs and data. Small systems do use magnetic tape cassettes or DEC tapes as mass-storage devices. All medium and large sized systems use a disk operating system (DOS).

Operating systems are usually designed as a set of modules that can be combined to form a complete operating system tailored to a specific hardware configuration. The system generation program usually supplied does this automatically, and systems generation is done only once for a configuration. The system is regenerated only when new hardware is added.

Disk Operating Systems

Disks have advantages over other mass-storage devices as the basis for an operating system. Because disks are random access devices, programs and data can be located and loaded more quickly than from serial devices. One physical disk drive can function as several logical devices by assigning areas of the disk to each logic device. For example, one area can be designated as the system device to store all system programs; other areas can be designated as intermediate storage for data and programs, as master file device, and as output device. Once transferred to the disk, programs can be executed at disk speeds rather than at the speed of the relatively slower I/O devices such as paper tape, magnetic tape, or keyboard. Eventually, the system must communicate with the outside world to obtain parameters and data from a paper tape or card reader and to produce a visual record via a printer.

Operator communication is through a keyboard/printer device, commonly a Teletype ASR or KSR 33, or a keyboard/printer with display. To make communication easy, operating systems have a control-language interpreter. The control language can consist of a few statements (messages formatted so as to be interpreted as directives) or as many as 40 or 50 statements. Control commands can be input by the operator from the keyboard to control the system directly; for automatic control, the system input device, which is usually a paper tape or card reader, is activated. To enter a job in the system, job control records are prepared, using appropriate control statements to interface them to the system.

The system output device is usually a printer for listings and reports. If a small amount of output is produced, a Teletype or other serial printer is used. If output is heavy, a fast line printer is used.

Most system programs run under DOS: assembler, language compilers, loader, and editor. The operating system calls the programs as needed and executes them in accordance with the programmer's instructions given in the job control statements. The assembler and compilers use the subroutine library to implement conversions between data formats and to perform needed arithmetic operations.

One important service supplied by the operating system is file management. A file is any group of computer words treated as a unit for input, storage, or output. The file may consist of programs or data. File management consists of provisions for creating and naming files, deleting files, adding items to an existing file, deleting or changing items in a file, and reading or writing files.

Because many different files can be stored on a disk, the operating system stores on it a directory that contains the location of all files. This arrangement means that the directory must be read into main memory each time a file is accessed. To make this unnecessary, the file management system has provisions for opening and closing files. Open files are those that are currently being used by the program; closed files are those not currently being used. This technique allows a small directory containing disk locations of the active (open) files to be stored in main memory and eliminates the need to read the directory on the disk except when a file is opened.

File management systems also provide for protecting files by using a system of access codes. Each user has a unique access code for the system and has protect codes associated with his files. File management and file protection are considerably more complex than this discussion indicates. They are implemented in many different ways in different operating systems. For example, file protection in a system where the goal is to prevent a user from inadvertently destroying someone else's file is quite different from file protection against sabotage. Also, file management in a system where users build a number of programs and periodically call them for execution is quite different from file management for an inquiry system.

Although disk operating systems for minicomputers are for general purposes and can be used in many ways, the methods for implementing certain features make them better for some applications than for others. The mainframe hardware also dictates to some extent the way in which features are implemented. In addition, manufacturers tend to refine the efficiency of operating systems designed for the most vigorously marketed applications.

Real-Time Operating Systems

Real-time systems are designed to respond to real-time events. They may be data acquisition systems that collect available data, process it, and produce reports. They may be monitoring systems that accept data, check it, and signal an operator if something out of the ordinary occurs. They may be systems that control measuring instruments or control devices. They can read data, check it, process it, produce reports, keep the operation going, and signal the operator only if an alarm situation arises. They may be data communication or time sharing systems. They range from the simple to the very complex.

One characteristic of real-time systems is that real-time events have priorities; some events are more time critical than others. The computer system must take care of the most time-critical events first, the second most critical second, and so on; no event can be ignored or lost. When discussing real-time systems, writers and speakers often say that the most time-critical events are the most important data. This is not true, for all events are important, and all must be taken into account. Because of this necessity to handle events within a real-time frame and because their occurrences are not always predictable, real-time systems use a computer system that can do the job under the worst possible conditions, which seldom if ever happens. Under ordinary operating conditions, the processor is idle part of the time, waiting for something to happen.

Another characteristic of real-time systems for many applications is that the system must always be operative. In some cases, the result of the system's going down (becoming inoperative) is danger to human life; this could occur if a control system for a chemical or power plant went down. Whatever the installation, shutdown is very expensive; for example, consider the cost of production-line control interruption. To protect these critical systems, back-up systems and standby power supplies are used to minimize the risk of system failure.

Because real-time systems must always operate and must always have excess processing power for safety, real-time operating systems generally provide foreground and background operating modes. Real-time event processing is done in a protected foreground mode. Program development, or even batch processing, is done in the unprotected background mode. The real-time system can be expanded or changed because real-time programs may be compiled, debugged, and tested thoroughly in the background before they are transferred to the foreground. Also, processing having no connection with the real-time system can be done.

All foreground programs have priority over the background program for processor time; the background job is halted when a real-time event occurs. Thus, the background program runs only during free time of the processor. The background monitor portion of the real-time operating system is similar to a disk or batch operating system.

Hardware features such as memory protection and a priority-oriented interrupt system are very important for real-time processing systems. Analog-to-digital and digital-to-analog converters and subsystems, digital I/O modules, and the processor I/O structure are also important. Ordinary processor peripherals are real-time devices, so a real-time system can be thought of as a system operating as a peripheral processor.

Some real-time operating systems keep all the real-time programs in a dedicated area of main memory, and background programs run only in left-over memory. More sophisticated systems store some real-time programs on the disk and keep them in main memory only while they are running. This allows more memory area to be used by the background jobs. If a real-time program must run and needs memory being used by the background job, the background job is stored on the disk and the real-time job is then loaded into the released memory space. When the real-time job is finished, it is stored on the disk, and the background job is read back into memory and resumes executing. Usually, a fixed-head disk is used to store the programs temporarily because of its high speed. Disks that store programs swapped in and out of memory are often called "swapping" disks.

Real-time systems range in size; some control a few devices and others control dozens, hundreds, or more than a thousand. Most interrupt systems do not provide enough interrupt levels to assign one level to each device; therefore the operating system includes a software priority interrupt system that is used for job scheduling.

The scheduling algorithm—a defined set of rules for doing an operation on the computer—is an important component of real-time systems. Programs can be run on demand from an outside event, at fixed intervals, at a particular time of day, or as a result of a combination of events and timed intervals.

LANGUAGES

The most common languages implemented are FORTRAN, BASIC, ALGOL, FOCAL, RPG, a COBOL-like language, and assembler. No one system implements all these languages, but most large manufacturers implement three or four of them.

Assemblers

Assembler languages are machine oriented. At their simplest, they provide a one-to-one correspondence between a mnemonic code and a machine language code. Mnemonics that sound like the operation performed are assigned to the instructions, making them easy to remember and to write. The programmer uses these mnemonics to program a problem. A few mnemonic codes are included to program pseudo-operations that direct the way a program is assembled. The assembler program translates mnemonic codes (source code) into an executable program written in machine language code (object code). The object code can be in absolute format; that is, addresses are assigned and it is always executed from the same locations in main memory.

An assembler enhancement is the production of the object code in relocatable format so that it can be loaded into and executed from any area in main memory. To do this, addresses are calculated relative to a base address, which is assigned when the program is loaded.

Other enhancements are often added to translate macro-instructions. A programmer can treat a macro-instruction like an additional machine language instruction, but it is actually composed of a number of instructions that perform a specific function. A macro-instruction is like a subroutine except that the assembler implements it differently. A subroutine is implemented by linking it to the subroutine code, which is located separately from the program in memory. A macro is assembled in line; that is, a number of instructions are substituted for the macro in the program.

The manufacturer can define macro-instructions for the system and include them in the assembler. Some assemblers also provide means for the user's defining of macros for a specific application. Once the programmer defines (programs) a macro, it is treated like a system macro, and the programmer can use it in the same way as a mnemonic instruction. Most systems allow the nesting of macros; that is, a macro can use another macro in its definition, which in turn can use a macro in its definition, and so on. Usually, the manufacturer limits the number of levels of nesting to four or six.

A sophisticated macro-assembler looks like a higher-level language compiler and requires 4K to 8K words of main memory for execution. Most manufacturers provide several versions of the assembler; the smaller versions implement subsets of the full assembler language for small systems with small main memory of 4K or 8K words.

Compilers

Compiler languages are more machine-independent than assemblers; ideally, they are completely machine-independent. The original idea was that programs written in a standard high-level language could be run on any computer that had a compiler (program) to convert the language statements into machine language code. Standard FORTRAN, and COBOL languages were defined by committees made up of computer users, federal government employees, and computer manufacturers. Others defined include ANSI FORTRAN and ANSI COBOL, versions defined by the American National Standards Institute (formerly the American Standards Association, or ASA). ALGOL, used internationally, was defined by the International Organization for Standardization (ISO), which is composed of members from the United States and western European countries. Despite its international use, ALGOL has not been adopted as a standard.

In the course of developing the current standard languages, a number of standards were formulated and revised. Standard FORTRAN, for example, is sometimes called FORTRAN IV because it is the fourth standard version.

Simultaneously, manufacturers implemented the languages and added or deleted features of the current version according to their own ideas and requirements. Because early applications for minicomputers were in scientific processing and the FORTRAN language is oriented toward this field, most minicomputer manufacturers implemented a version of FORTRAN. Basic FORTRAN or FORTRAN II was usually used. In the past few years, however, due primarily to the availability of inexpensive disks for minicomputers, manufacturers have implemented FORTRAN IV or ANSI FORTRAN.

ALGOL is also oriented toward scientific processing, but is better than FORTRAN for commercial processing. It is also a popular language in western Europe. Some minicomputer manufacturers who market abroad extensively implement ALGOL compilers, although ALGOL does not define input/output and therefore each compiler language must define its own.

The early hope that programs written in a standard higher-level language could run on any system that implements the language has not been realized. The federal government exerts pressure on the computer industry by specifying standards for the systems it buys. The Navy, for example, has a program to validate COBOL compilers. So far, only a few have been certified as meeting the ANSI COBOL standard.

The Office of Information Processing Standards of the National Bureau of Standards has been working since 1967 on routines that can be used to validate ANSI FORTRAN compilers. These 116 routines were released in April 1973. Manufacturers wishing to validate their own compilers will be able to buy the routines for a nominal fee.

Frequently, a manufacturer will make computers that are not program-compatible at the assembler language level but are program-compatible for higher-level languages. Generally, minicomputers made by one manufacturer are neither assembly language compatible nor higher-level language compatible with those made by any other manufacturer. There are a few exceptions, however, where a manufacturer deliberately designs and markets a system that is program-compatible with a popular minicomputer. The IBM 1130 and 1800, DEC PDP-8 and Data General's Nova 1200 have program-compatible counterparts made by other manufacturers. Because the imitator does not spend time and money in developing system software, he can sell his system more cheaply than the original manufacturer. Generally, he can sell his system only to users who have at least one system from the original manufacturer, thus giving the user legitimate access to the system software. When design pirating occurs, the original minicomputer manufacturer can sue the imitator; a number of such cases are still pending. The solution of this problem has not yet been clarified legally, but manufacturers will undoubtedly take steps to protect their new system software from this kind of use. So far, however, the imitators have been quite successful.

Basic FORTRAN compilers are sometimes available to run on systems that are too small to support an operating system, but other compilers are usually designed to run under the batch or disk operating system or under the background monitor of a real-time operating system. Compilers have extensive checking features to diagnose programmer errors in the use of the language, either errors in semantics (meaning) or syntax (form). In practice, most errors detected are errors in syntax. Error messages that contain the statement line in error and an error code to indicate the error type are printed out on the system output device. The programmer can use the error messages to correct the source code so that the program can be recompiled into executable object code. The program is listed and the program stored on a mass-storage device from which it can be read and executed. A common feature is an optional compile-and-go; that is, as soon as the program is successfully compiled, it is executed.

Occasionally a FORTRAN compiler may be run in the interpretive mode. In this mode, each statement is individually compiled and the instructions executed without producing an object program. This might be used if a person were to utilize the minicomputer as a desk calculator.

The BASIC and FOCAL compilers are usually called interpreters rather than compilers because they run in the interpretive mode. These interpreters generally have an optional compile mode; that is, they can produce executable object code, which can be listed and stored for later use.

Most minicomputer time-sharing systems use the BASIC language. Digital

Equipment Corporation (DEC) also uses FOCAL because it was an early DEC development before BASIC became popular, and many users of DEC equipment like it better than BASIC. In fact, FOCAL users are loyal and vocal. At a DECUS (Digital Equipment Users' Society) meeting in May 1972, a debate was scheduled on the merits of FOCAL versus BASIC as a desk calculator language. The debate was well attended and it became so heated that even King Solomon could not have rendered a clear-cut decision for one language over the other. In any case, DEC implements FOCAL as well as BASIC for its computer systems, so users can choose whichever they prefer.

To date, BASIC and FOCAL have not acquired the status of standardized languages, but a movement is beginning to standardize BASIC, a development that will probably happen in the next few years. Many versions of FOCAL have been implemented, particularly for the PDP-8.

Appendixes A, B, C and D describe the FORTRAN, ALGOL, BASIC, and FOCAL languages in more detail.

A few systems implement RPG. This is not a standard language but is implemented according to the manufacturers' own specifications. Although the language is designed primarily to simplify report generation, it does have data processing facilities to generate the entries in reports.

For commercial data processing, a COBOL-like language is occasionally offered. Among these versions is DEC, which provides DIBOL for its commercial systems for the PDP-8 (Fig. 4-1). Honeywell provides Level 1 COBOL for its 1640 series of time-sharing systems. Standard COBOL provides three levels for its implementation; Level 1 is the most abbreviated version.

Other languages that are oriented toward a particular application are often offered. For example, Honeywell offers TEACH, a string processing language for producing computer-aided instruction training materials. Data General offers Datapoint, a language for developing parts specification programs.

APPLICATIONS SOFTWARE

All manufacturers have some applications software for their systems. A wealth of applications software is available for many systems that are upward compatible with older systems, such as the DEC PDP-8/E, Honeywell's System 700, and Hewlett Packard's 2100A. Dozens of applications packages are available for older systems such as the IBM 1800 and 1130. The applications span a broad range, from subroutines for trigometric functions to inventory control. In addition, the users of equipment from the larger manufacturers have formed users' groups that meet periodically to discuss hardware, software, and applications. For example, DECUS main-

tains a library of routines submitted to it by users and issues newsletters
for communication among users.

FIG. 4-1.   DEC DATASYSTEM-330, built around PDP-8 computer, self-contained system; designed to solve variety of accounting and information reporting
problems.

5. MINICOMPUTER APPLICATIONS

Minicomputers are used in five broadly definable application areas: industrial process control, peripheral control, computation, data acquisition, and communications.

INDUSTRIAL PROCESS CONTROL

Systems for industrial control have provided the largest percentage of minicomputer industry sales. In this application area, minicomputers serve to control industrial processes, to direct numerically controlled machine tools, to operate equipment such as automatic typesetters, and to test systems, subsystems, and components both for quality control on the production line and for monitoring and maintenance in the field.

Minicomputers are found in almost every type of industry and are used for everything from incoming material inspection, through quality control testing, to final packaging and inventory control.

Each minicomputer application, whether in the chemical, pharmaceutical, petroleum, electronics, food, or apparel industries, requires a mathematical model of the process to be controlled. The minicomputer monitors the signals of the process control instrumentation, performs the required data processing, and outputs correction signals, either to the process control equipment directly or to an operation or manual implementation.

Although users in these industries are usually well versed in their particular technology, their backgrounds in EDP are frequently marginal.

Because the application requires development of a mathematical model, instrumentation, computer interfaces, and application programs, the system vendor is often forced into a lengthy role as advisor. The manufacturer—or the OEM (original equipment manufacturer) or the system assembler—must also provide extensive system software such as operating systems, utility and diagnostic routines, and I/O routines. In some cases the user will buy a minicomputer system only if it is offered complete with an application software package.

In most industrial applications, the minicomputer with its peripherals and software costs less than the process instrumentation, computer interfaces, and control equipment. Despite its relatively low cost, the minicomputer performs functions that are critical, so it must satisfy the highest standards of reliability. At best, a malfunctioning minicomputer can ruin a batch of chemicals. At worst, a malfunction can adversely affect or even jeopardize the lives of millions of people.

Minicomputers often are more reliable than traditional electromechanical control systems. Minicomputer-based process control can integrate control of complex systems in a way that traditional designs rarely can match. In addition, minicomputers have the potential for comprehensive in-process self-testing, and can increase or decrease accuracy if required by system drift or aging. Finally, minicomputers are readily adaptable to changes in materials or processes because only the software need be changed.

Application Profile: Industrial Control

Company A buys minicomputers OEM for use in the process control systems that it sells to end users, often on a turnkey basis. The four-year-old company employs 130 people. It was established initially to sell systems to one specific process industry, but later branched out to broader markets.

This firm uses the minicomputer as the main processor in its control systems. In addition to special interfaces, process instrumentation (which the company makes itself, for the most part), and computer peripherals (including terminals and displays), this firm provides software, custom design, and installation as a total package. The resulting modular systems are structured to meet the unique needs of each end user.

The minicomputer obtains signals from many process sensors, applies them to a computer-stored mathematical model of the process, and outputs corrective signals to process controllers. Certain data is logged and displayed for monitoring by the operators, for further refinement of the process and its associated control systems, and for production reporting.

A clear-cut need for flexibility at modest cost makes alternatives to a minicomputer unrealistic for this firm.

Over 10 man-years have been invested by this company in software development. When selecting a minicomputer, the six largest vendors were initially considered. The final choice was made on the basis of reliability, quality, manufacturer reputation, software support, and service.

Company A also uses in-house minicomputers for engineering analysis, production control, gauge inspection, and components checkout.

PERIPHERAL CONTROL

In peripheral control applications, minicomputers have been used to control terminals, data entry systems, or computer input/output devices. Minicomputers supplant hard-wired controllers when flexibility and adaptability to a broad range of devices are required. They are used instead of the main computer for peripheral control when the main processor performance needs to be improved. The minicomputer's ability to service interrupts, control input/output and perform sequencing, data transfers, buffering, editing, and formatting make it well suited to this task.

Users in this application area generally have extensive technical knowledge and broad experience in the design and use of computers. They know from direct experience that minicomputer-based peripheral control systems often require expensive interfaces that typically cost as much as the mini itself. They also know that the manufacturer will provide little support at the price they are willing to pay for the system. The burden of designing the overall system, and of adapting and programming the selected minicomputer, falls on the minicomputer buyer.

Application Profile: Peripheral Control

Company B manufactures computer disk storage drives, displays, and specialized computer systems. The company buys minicomputers OEM to use as controllers for the peripheral equipment it manufactures. System configurations that it sells to end users and other OEMs vary but include some data input/output devices, and storage, interface, and communication devices. The minicomputer is often connected to a larger main computer at the customer's site. The mini provides block data transfers, editing, and similar functions, and takes some load off the main computer. Only modest system-oriented software is supplied by the company.

Company B ruled out the use of the host computer to control its peripheral devices because it typically lacks the proper software to drive the firm's display system. Also, from an economic standpoint, the reduced overhead on the main computer more than recovers the price of the mini. Hard-wired equipment was tried experimentally, but was found unacceptable because of its inflexibility.

Formal analysis was used for the company's minicomputer selection. The analysis considered hardware specifications, price/performance, and pricing policies as the most important criteria, followed by reliability, service, and field maintenance capability of the suppliers.

The company also uses in-house minicomputers for some of its manufacturing applications, including checkout of disk units and complete systems.

COMPUTATION

In this application, minicomputers are used for business, financial, and scientific data processing, primarily in new markets that could not afford EDP until the advent of the minicomputer. The minicomputers are also used in time-sharing networks, servicing a number of users simultaneously.

Minicomputers are used in places where cost is an overriding consideration; for example, in small companies and educational institutions. They are also used in rather large operations, including manufacturing plants, research and development, engineering, and consulting organizations. In their various computing applications, minicomputers accept input data from peripheral equipment, process it in accordance with their prestored programs, and output the results via printers or displays. They assemble and compile programs or operate as a desk calculator for multiple time-sharing users.

In these roles, the minicomputer replaces manual/electromechanical computation or inefficient (and often inconvenient) use of a large batch processing or time-sharing computer. The mini's advantages are its low cost, ease of operation, and accessibility to the individual user. These advantages more than offset its size limitations.

Application Profile: Computation

A small liberal arts college installed a minicomputer approximately two years ago for educational purposes. It includes a mark-sense card reader, a Teletype ASR 33, and a minicomputer central processor with 12,000 words of memory plus necessary interfaces. Purchase price of this system is approximately $23,000.

This system is used 6 or 7 hours per day for student instruction. It assembles and executes student-written programs of a diverse nature. When demand for time on this system increases substantially, the college will consider a commercial time-sharing service, but at the present time it would be substantially more expensive.

In selecting a minicomputer, several of the systems from larger manufacturers were considered. Manufacturer reputation and financial stability were significant factors in the evaluation. Price/performance, reliability, freedom from being locked in to future equipment purchases, software support, and geographical location were the selection criteria used. An important advantage of the selected computer was that it was specifically marketed in the education field. The manufacturer was willing and able to give strong support to customers in this area.

DATA ACQUISITION

Minicomputers are widely used for data acquisition in many industrial and military applications, research and development organizations, hospitals, and laboratories. They accept data from multiple sources, often at high transfer rates, and then store, log, edit, format, and preprocess it. The data can come from experimental process control instruments, test or measuring devices, satellites, or specialized peripheral equipment. In such applications, the minicomputer offers flexibility, high speed, low cost, and excellent price/performance as attractive alternatives to the hard-wired devices and larger computers commonly used for data acquisition.

The cost of the interfaces and peripheral equipment that are typically required are much higher than system design and programming costs. These latter costs are relatively low, even though the user (because of the unique nature of most such systems) must design and implement the system and develop the application software. Most users in this area have extensive technical and EDP backgrounds and can do their own programming, using the languages and system software supplied with the minicomputer.

Application Profile: Data Acquisition

A laboratory that is a joint venture by a major university and the Atomic Energy Commission is a user of minicomputers for data acquisition. Its principal function is to operate a 2-mile long atomic particle accelerator for a variety of research experiments in the field of atomic physics. It has a permanent staff of approximately 1000 people. Its main computer center is very large, includes a large-scale IBM System/360 and eight medium-sized computers, which are used to process great volumes of data involving highly complex computations.

Of the several minicomputers used at the site, four are used for on-line data acquisition. Configured and adapted for various experiments, these systems gather data at high speeds and store it for later processing at the main computer center. Individual experiments are generally of short duration (a few days to a few weeks) and require a maximum of one man-month per experiment for the programming that is unique to the particular experiment. The laboratory has a large, well-qualified, in-house staff for software development.

Time sharing is too expensive for the laboratory. Hardwiring is unsuitable because the system must be adaptable for each successive experiment.

In selecting a minicomputer, only major companies that had an established reputation (of at least two years) were considered. The laboratory established its own system specification and then compared each vendor's product. The most important selection criteria were hardware specifications, price/performance, reliability, quality, and documentation.

COMMUNICATIONS

Data communications is one of the fastest-growing applications for minicomputers. Typical functions include line concentration to reduce the number of long transmission lines, message-flow control in switching centers, and front-end communication control for large computers. As a line concentrator the minicomputer receives data on several low-speed lines, interleaves characters, and transmits the packed data on a single high-speed line. In message switching, the minicomputer accepts messages from multiple sources, logs the messages, routes them to multiple output lines, and verifies their transmission. Minicomputers used as communication front ends for large computers perform line control functions, monitoring, editing, and formatting incoming messages.

Typical applications that use minicomputers for data communications include airline ticket and hotel room reservation systems, stock quotation systems, intra- or interplant message systems for large companies, and internal communications at EDP sites.

The traditional approach for these functions has been to use either hard-wired devices, a small computer, or even a large computer. A minicomputer, however, offers greater flexibility and adaptability than do the hard-wired devices, and costs substantially less than either the small or large computer.

Application Profile: Communications

Company C is one of the larger commercial time-sharing firms in the United States. Its nationwide time-sharing system provides computational capability for many users who apply this to a variety of scientific and business applications. As an end user, the company has purchased approximately 60 minicomputers for use in its time-sharing network. These minis perform several functions, including error detection/retransmission, editing, formatting, and adjusting for code and speed differences between the remote terminals, communication lines, and the central time-sharing computers.

According to the company, there are no acceptable alternatives to minicomputers. Without minis, the central computers would be overburdened, leading to an unacceptable drop in the number of users that are served and a corresponding decrease in revenue. Flexibility would be severely reduced, affecting the types and number of terminals available, transmission speeds, accuracy of data transmission, and line costs.

The company prefers to do all its own software development and has a large, highly qualified staff for this purpose. Many man-years have already been invested in a continuing software development program.

Its original list of potential minicomputer suppliers included five of the largest firms. Final selection criteria placed greatest emphasis upon cost, reliability, equipment architecture, word length, and delivery. The company performs a 30-day "burn in" on each new mini to establish reliability; it has personnel trained in circuit design and in-house fabrication, and can produce custom-made interfaces and engineering changes to its minicomputer communication systems.

6. SELECTING A MINICOMPUTER

There are many ways to select a minicomputer, but a purchaser should use a method that reflects his chief concerns. Some users consider price alone, given a certain minimum level of machine performance. Others are primarily concerned with performance, especially if some potential applications are still imperfectly defined; they are willing to pay a high premium to offset future difficulties. Still others, OEMs and system assemblers typically, know their needs precisely, but often buy an older machine that is more expensive in terms of price/performance than more recent models because they have a large investment in software developed for that particular minicomputer.

COMPETING ALTERNATIVES

Before proceeding into an extensive evaluation of minicomputer systems, the potential user must decide whether a minicomputer is the most desirable solution for his particular problem. For most problems, there are alternatives available. Three alternatives are usually competitive with minicomputers: wired logic, large computers, and commercial time sharing (CTS).

Wired Logic

Wired logic is the use of hard-wired components and circuits designed to perform a specific predesigned function. To change the function, the wired connections within the system structure must be reconnected. Wired logic is the hardware approach to problem solution, whereas a minicomputer is a software approach. In other words, wired-logic control is in the electronic circuits and minicomputer control is in a stored computer program that can be changed by loading a new program.

Wired logic has two major advantages over minicomputers. It costs less because only the minimum required functions are built into the systems, and it is faster. A relatively high proportion of its cost is in the labor for its design. Because labor costs are continually increasing and minicomputer prices are declining, the cost advantage of wired logic tends to decline with time. On the other hand, low-cost MSI/LSI circuits for wired-logic control are available for very high-volume applications that require identical logic modules. The primary weakness of wired logic is its inflexibility. Any change whatsoever necessitates redesign and reconstruction of the system.

In some cases, minicomputers differ little from wired logic because they can be built with fixed programs stored in read-only memory. This type of configuration is properly classified as both a minicomputer and a wired-logic controller.

Large Computers

Relative to minicomputers a large computer is one that sells for more than $25,000 in its basic configuration. In this sense, IBM System/3 is a large computer. A large computer is an alternative to a minicomputer, either as a direct replacement or as a shared machine. If it is a direct replacement, the choice is relatively straightforward. The added cost of the large computer is justified only if the capacity requirements of the application cannot be satisfied by the minicomputer system. The capacity of the shared large computer is distributed over many applications, one or more of which can be performed by a separate minicomputer. For example, an engineering laboratory could use a dedicated stand-alone mini for scientific computation or it could use a central system that does data processing for all types of applications within the company.

The choice between a shared computer and a mini reflects the problem of centralized computation versus distributed computation. Many variables such as access to the computer, response time, computational capacity, memory capacity, the type of processing, and intangible factors affect the decision in a particular application. General guidelines are difficult to produce; each application must be considered on its own merits.

Commercial Time Sharing

Commercial time-sharing (CTS) systems use a large centralized computing facility that services a multitude of remotely located terminals. These systems handle several remote users concurrently so that each user ideally appears to have complete use of the large centralized computer to himself at any given time. The CTS system has grown rapidly in the past few years. It has been used primarily for engineering and scientific computation, but the suppliers have expanded into business applications and special information systems such as financial data.

Economic advantages to low-volume users are better response times, and relatively large computational and memory capacities. The primary weaknesses of CTS are its cost for high-volume users, low input/output data rates, operational problems with the communication system, system reliability, potential degradation of response times in peak hours, and removal of operational control from the user.

Comparison with Minicomputers

A comparison of the three competing alternatives with minicomputers in each of the five application areas is outlined in Tables 4-1 to 4-3. Based on the factors indicated in these tables, the following list summarizes the comparison of each alternative with minicomputers by application area:

Industrial control: Minicomputers are usually the most desirable approach bcause of their flexibility.

Peripheral control: Wired logic is a lower-cost approach and should remain most prevalent, although declining costs should make minicomputers increasingly desirable.

Computation: Minicomputer manufacturers have a limited capability to market to the potential users, as well as limited software and system support. Hence, the use of small business computers such as the IBM System/3, commercial time sharing, larger computer systems, or electronic accounting machines are frequently more desirable approaches.

Data acquisition: Minicomputers are usually the most desirable approach because of their flexibility.

Communications: Time-division multiplex (TDM) and frequency-division multiplex (FDM) switches, and I/O controllers are more desirable in many communication applications.

Table 4-1. Comparison of Wired Logic with Minicomputers

Industrial control	Minicomputer advantages are flexibility to modify control procedures and to adjust process parameters, greater analytical capabilities for decision making, and greater understanding of the process which results from the analysis associated with implementing the minicomputer system.
Peripheral control	Wired logic is most frequent type of controller especially for low-cost peripherals. Speed of wired logic is needed for applications with very high data rates. Minicomputer should gain favor with larger peripherals requiring flexible control. When used in remote terminals, minicomputers provide several advantages: lower communication costs due to data reduction and high-speed transmission; reduction in the transmission of erroneous data due to pre-editing; more efficient data editing with a small computer rather than a large central computer.
Computation	Wired logic is very limited in computational capabilities and flexibility. Wired logic provides alternative only for very low computation loads, as in desk calculators. There is limited effect on all three areas of minicomputer computational use—in-house time sharing, scientific computation, and business data processing.
Data acquisition	Wired logic is a potential alternative due to low cost. However, flexibility provided by minicomputer is a strong advantage.
Communications	Time-division and frequency-division switches are commonly used instead of minis for multiplexers. Special-purpose I/O controllers are used instead of minis as front-end communication devices. Mini provides greater flexibility.

MINICOMPUTER SELECTION

After deciding that a minicomputer is most appropriate for an application, the next problem is in selecting the particular machine. In evaluating a minicomputer, the potential purchaser should examine four main areas:

1. The technical and architectural comparison of the machine to others in its category.

2. Any features or capabilities that are especially relevant to the intended applications.

3. The available software, both system software and software packages directly or closely related to the intended applications.

Table 4-2. Comparison of Large Computers with Minicomputers

Industrial control	The capacity of a dedicated large computer is usually not required. Sharing of a large computer with other tasks requires frequent monitoring of sensors and is generally an inefficient use of the large computer's capacity due to interrupt processing overhead.
Peripheral control	Large computers are frequently used to control their on-line peripherals. Separate controllers are most desirable for high-speed and multiple low-speed devices and in those cases requiring special data structuring or formatting functions.
Computation	The large computer is a definite alternative to the minicomputer in large organizations which already have a central computer installation. However, it is not a serious alternative in a small organization. A large CPU offers advantages of more computations per dollar, availability of large data base, and larger I/O capacity. The minicomputer offers advantages of faster response time, greater accessibility, and more efficient execution of preprocessing tasks such as data editing, checking, and formatting. The most significant impact in this area will come from IBM's System/3 which is a small system but not strictly a minicomputer. Due to IBM's marketing capability, System/3 is expected to gain the majority of small business applications.
Data acquisition	The large computer is required for special, very high-volume data transfer rates. However, minicomputers are capable of handling a large majority of the potential market at significantly lower costs.
Communications	A front-end minicomputer is usually a desirable subsystem in a communications-oriented computer system. The line monitoring functions, which involve interrupt processing overhead, are more efficiently assigned to a low-cost communications processor rather than a large central computer.

4. The manufacturer's reputation, his experience with similar installations, and the quality and extent of his service and support organization.

Few of these factors can be precisely reduced to numbers, and any good evaluation is inherently subjective. Nevertheless, factual data such as a minicomputer's word length, memory size, and the size and nature of its instruction set, among others, are important, for lack of any one may make a particular computer impractical for application. Therefore, the manufacturer's specification sheet should be studied in detail.

Table 4-3. Comparison of Commercial Time Sharing (CTS) with Minicomputers

Industrial control	CTS is not feasible because of unacceptable response times, low data rates, inadequate interfaces, and inadequate system reliability.
Peripheral control	CTS is not appropriate for peripheral control.
Computation	CTS is the strongest competitor to minicomputers in this application area. CTS competes in all three areas of computational use—in-house time sharing, scientific computation, and business data processing. CTS has been used most widely for scientific and engineering computation. Recently, business application services have been expanded by CTS companies. The tradeoff between CTS and a free-standing mini depends on the level of use—generally CTS will be more expensive for over 30-50 hours computer time per month. CTS offers the advantage of a large data base capability but presents problems with the communications systems, gaining access to the system in peak hours, response time in peak hours, security of information, and limited I/O capabilities due to limitations of available terminals. In-house time sharing is more cost-effective than CTS for a multiple terminal user with a small data base requirement.
Data acquisition	CTS is not an appropriate alternative.
Communications	CTS is a feasible alternative in only very limited situations, i.e., cases in which CTS service is used as a substitute for an in-house communications system.

Technical Comparison

The various design features of minicomputers interact in complex ways to yield an overall level of performance capability for a machine. No universal way of evaluating these features exists because the performance of a computer must be measured against the specific application requirements. Nevertheless, a fast comparison of the technical specifications of available minicomputers will provide an initial indication of relative performance. Minicomputer technology has been yielding rapid improvements in performance. Therefore, the user should be sure he is buying a machine that is competitive in its performance capabilities.

The features to be analyzed in the initial technical comparison should include:

Word length: Longer word length machines are more expensive but are more efficient because they require fewer memory accesses and retrieve more information per access.

Machine speed: Memory cycle time is a basic indicator of execution speed. Typical minicomputers offer cycle times of 0.8 to 2.0 μs. For applications having high computational loads, machines with cycle times in the range of 300 to 400 ns are available with semiconductor memories. Several other characteristics must be analyzed to evaluate machine speed. How many memory cycles are required to execute an instruction? Does the machine overlap instruction fetching and execution? Does the machine offer a high-speed scratchpad memory that can be used for fast execution of high-frequency programs or program loops? One method for measuring machine speed is to run benchmark problems that are representative of the user's particular application.

Availability of general-purpose registers: The declining cost of semi-conductors has led to increased availability of general-purpose registers in minicomputers. These registers can be used as accumulators, temporary storage locations, stack pointers, or index registers; all make programming easier. The availability of these registers in hardware as opposed to main memory reduces memory accesses and improves execution speed.

Instruction set: Minicomputers offer a wide range of options in available instructions. Some machines offer only basic instructions (such as LOAD, ADD, SUBTRACT) and require lengthy sequences to implement programs. Others, using a microprogrammed design, offer complex instructions specifically designed for given applications. Machines using a microprogrammed design typically are more expensive, but they often improve price/performance through higher processing efficiency for a given application.

Input/output control: In many applications the limiting factor on machine capability is its input/output transfer rate. The transfer requirements of the intended application should be well defined and the buyer should insure that a machine can satisfy this requirement.

Interrupt efficiency: Many applications require frequent data exchange with the external environment. For these applications a machine that processes interrupts quickly and offers multilevel priorities is desirable.

Memory capacity: Some minicomputers are limited in the maximum main memory available. Hence, the buyer should determine his main memory requirements to insure that a given machine can satisfy them.

Available peripherals: Minicomputers vary widely in the range of available peripherals. The buyer should determine the input/output loads and storage requirements of the intended applications and determine which machines offer peripherals to satisfy these requirements.

Evaluation of Application Features

Next it is necessary to consider the match between the mini's capabilities and the user's requirements. The most important requirements within each application area usually are:

Industrial control: high reliability, flexible I/O structure, extensive interrupt capability, good system software, addressing flexibility, memory protection, high peripheral I/O transfer rates, FORTRAN capability, flexible I/O handling routines, available mathematical routines, diagnostic software.

Peripheral control: flexible I/O structure, extensive interrupt and communication capabilities, and good addressing capability.

Computation: ease of operator use, large memory and auxiliary storage capability, extensive range of peripherals, extensive system and application software (especially easily learned languages), a FORTRAN compiler, an extensive instruction set, scientific and mathematical routines, user-oriented I/O software, a multiprogramming operating system.

Data acquisition: high I/O rates and efficient I/O structure, large memory and auxiliary storage capacity, short memory cycle time, software with data-manipulation capabilities.

Communications: byte-oriented instructions, efficient interrupt structure, flexible I/O structure, high system throughput, short memory cycle time, good reliability, extensive system software (including a good operating system), an assembly language with a macro capability, and a bit-manipulation capability.

Software Evaluation

Software development for specific applications is the most frequently underestimated item in an EDP budget. In fact, the high cost of software development, along with the equally high cost of peripherals, is at the top of the list of typical user complaints.

It is very desirable that the minicomputer supplier provide application packages that are well matched to the intended applications. These packages can reduce startup time and the size of the required EDP staff. Such software packages, having already been tested for usefulness in the real-world environment, frequently prove to be more comprehensive and adaptable than programs developed in house. Also, any increase in system price associated with such software will be minor compared to the cost of user-developed software because development cost is amortized over many users.

The availability of good system software is important for efficient program development. System software should include diagnostic routines for system maintenance. Tests should be provided to check the operation of every unit in the system and to diagnose malfunctions. The kind of software adaptable to the user's system depends on his hardware configuration. Some software requires mass storage such as magnetic tape, drum, or disk.

Many manufacturers provide modular software, with each module requiring a specific, minimum hardware configuration.

Generally, developing and running programs on a small hardware configuration is harder than on a larger system because less system software is provided, the facilities in the compiler languages are less elegant, and the system is less automatic and requires more operator intervention. Small hardware configurations lend themselves more readily to applications where the same tasks are performed repeatedly. Because programs do require changing from time to time, however, even the smallest hardware configuration should have facilities for changing programs and for developing programs and incorporating them in the system.

Utility routines should be supplied to debug source code and edit output code. Input/output handlers should be provided. Loaders should be furnished to load all software supplied with the system and to load application programs.

Assemblers   System software universally includes an assembler. Because the assembler is probably the most important software package supplied, the assembler features should be evaluated with care. Many manufacturers supply more than one assembler for different hardware configurations, with the assembly language for a small configuration being a subset of the assembly language designed for a larger configuration.

The following assembly features should be compared:

1. Number of passes of the source code.
2. Number of core locations occupied by the assembler program.
3. The number and types of diagnostic message outputs.
4. Pseudo-operation codes provided.
5. Whether the output code from an assembly is in fixed, binary format, or in relocatable format.

6. The number and types of macros provided in the assembly language.
7. Whether the assembly language includes facilities for incorporating user-defined macros.
8. The extent to which macros can be nested.

The user should be concerned with ease and speed with which application programs can be coded, debugged, and run on the system. The problem lies in how to translate specific application needs into desired assembler characteristics.

Most assemblers require a minimum of two passes of the source code to produce an assembled program; so-called one-pass assemblers either leave many references to be resolved by a loader or are really two-pass assemblers that do not require the source code to be read twice from the source code input device. The first pass checks the source code for syntactic errors and builds the symbol table in memory. The second pass completes the assembly and tags unresolved references for the loader.

For small configurations, one selection criterion should be the number of times the tape reader must be loaded before the program is executed. For larger systems with mass storage, this is not a problem.

The number of core locations required by the assembler, subtracted from the total number of core locations in the system, defines the maximum size of the symbol table, which indirectly determines the length of programs that can be assembled. Symbols are data and program tags or labels. For short-word-length computers, each entry in the symbol table probably requires more than one word.

Psuedo-operation codes do not generate machine-language output code but direct the assembly program to define data, specify conditional assembly, equate labels, and so on. The data definition pseudo-operations are especially important if the application areas require different data formats. The data formats provided should correspond to those required by the applications.

The number and type of diagnostic messages that a system can output determine the ease with which source code can be debugged. Most assemblers combine two or more error types in some of the diagnostic messages printed out with the statement of the error and its location in core. Users must be wary of diagnostic messages in which many errors are tied to one message. These indicate little more than the fact that an error was made.

A relocatable assembler produces machine-language output code relative to a base address. When the assembled program is loaded for execution, the loader adds the base address appropriate for the current memory map; thus, the program can be stored and run anywhere in memory.

A fixed, binary assembler produces output code that must always be loaded and executed in the same area of memory; this is a considerably less flexible arrangement.

A macro-assembler treats certain functions that require several machine-language instructions for execution as one instruction. The assembler takes one source-language statement, generates all the instructions needed to implement the statement, and inserts the group of instructions into the output code. Macros make programming in assembly language easier and make source-language programs shorter and less subject to error.

The ability to incorporate user-defined macros into the assembly program is a powerful tool for tailoring an assembler to a specific application. Frequently required functions can be programmed and incorporated into the assembler and thereafter treated as system macros.

The extent to which macros can be nested determines the ease of programming user-defined macros, particularly complex ones. Nesting macros means that one macro can use another macro in its definition, the second macro can use a third macro in its definition, and so on up to the number of levels allowed. This facility is important if different, complex application programs have simpler functions in common that can be constructed into complex ones.

Another important characteristic of an assembler is its assembly speed. For applications where the same programs are run repeatedly, the assembly speed is of little importance, but if different newer and shorter problems will be run, assembly speed is significant. Determining the assembly speed is difficult, so the best information source is another user.

Compilers   Evaluating compilers is similar to evaluating assemblers; the assessment must reflect the needs of the application. The most common higher-level language offered with minicomputers is FORTRAN. Currently, two FORTRAN languages are defined by ANSI (American National Standards Institute); these are Basic FORTRAN (formerly FORTRAN II) and Standard FORTRAN (formerly FORTRAN IV). Despite efforts at standardization, FORTRAN compilers remain machine-oriented, that is, programs written for one system will not necessarily run on another system.

A FORTRAN compiler for a particular system either does not include all features of a standard FORTRAN language or does include additional features not defined in the standard FORTRAN language. Compilers should be evaluated with respect to application-oriented criteria by comparing those features offered by the language with those desirable in the intended applications.

As with assemblers, other important features are the hardware configuration required, the main memory occupied by the compiler, the maximum size program that can be compiled, and the number and kind of diagnostic messages output. An important compiler criterion is the efficiency of the output code, but this is difficult to evaluate without running benchmark problems. In addition, compilers should allow the incorporation of assembly language subroutines.

For small systems with only a Teletype ASR 33 or ASR 35 for input/output, the number of times the operator must load the paper tape reader and perform other mechanical operations indicates the relative convenience of running the compiler.

Operating Systems

Operating systems for minicomputers are becoming increasingly important, particularly for systems that include mass-storage devices. Most operating systems are of the foreground/background type; one or more real-time programs can be executed in the foreground. Time-sharing operating systems for minicomputers are also available.

Foreground/background operating systems make minicomputers suitable for real-time control applications and increase the overall efficiency of the computing system. Real-time programs are incorporated into the operating system and are executed in the foreground while batch programs can be executed during leftover processor time in the background. The important feature of these systems in control applications is that new, real-time programs can be debugged and prepared for incorporation in the operating system without closing down other ongoing programs.

Time-sharing operating systems are a variation of the foreground/background operating systems. Instead of real-time control programs being executed in the foreground, time-sharing users execute their programs in the foreground while batch programs run in the background.

In designing the operating system, the manufacturer makes various assumptions on which the system is based. These assumptions or system parameters reflect the system hardware and the application for which the hardware will be used. They include the average core storage required by a foreground or background problem, the maximum number of foreground problems, the maximum number of priority levels allowed, the type of programs that can be run in the foreground and background, the system software available to a user, and other parameters. Thus, a particular operating system can be too big and complex, too small and simplistic, or about right for a particular application, depending on the parameters used in the system design. An evaluation of a particular minicomputer should compare the operating system facilities required by the intended application to those actually provided by the minicomputer.

Qualifications of the Manufacturer

The characteristics attributed to the manufacturer supplying the system are important in selection because users require many services that will be contingent on manufacturer stability. The following factors should be considered:

1. Delivery schedules and reputation for meeting them.
2. Maintenance; distance of the computer site from the manufacturer or service center.
3. Response time to service calls.
4. Software support available for application programming.
5. Number of systems delivered.
6. Quality of documentation on hardware and software.
7. Training provided.
8. Financial stability.

The past performance of a vendor is best gauged by speaking to others who have bought his products. Most vendors will be glad to supply a list of users as references, and even the most satisfied user will be a good source of information on the comparative merits of competitive vendors. To some extent, the length of time a company has been in business is a guide to its success, its future durability, and, as a result, its ability to respond to a user's future needs. A new product, however, can have bugs even if it is introduced by an established vendor, so it is important to know that the system has been in use long enough to have been debugged.

When investigating a vendor, a user should try to determine who actually manufactures the minicomputer and whether the manufacturer also sells minis to other manufacturers (OEMs). A significant OEM market can be a plus factor for the vendor because it expands a manufacturer's production volume, lowers his costs, and improves his profitability via a more positive cash flow. As a result, the manufacturer is sounder financially and has greater probability of survival. In addition, OEMs tend to make more technical demands than do end users. Consequently, a manufacturer's involvement with OEM business leads to increased technical expertise and continued product improvements.

Good maintenance facilities, especially a fully staffed and stocked service center that is nearby, are important in getting the prompt and effective service required at some time by every minicomputer. Response time to a request for service is often a simple matter of geography, and in certain applications every minute of computer downtime may be costly.

A number of vendors do not have their own maintenance facilities. They contract with third-party firms to provide installation and maintenance service. This type of arrangement is a fairly recent innovation. According to users who are familiar with both types, third-party maintenance firms generally offer service of the same quality as that received from a vendor's own maintenance personnel.

The support a user can expect from a vendor is sometimes based on a contractual agreement, but more generally it is a reflection of the vendor's policy with regard to customers. Several factors are involved. A large company can usually offer much more support to users than can a small company. A small company, however, may be more anxious for the sale and therefore more willing to commit itself to an extended period of support services, including assistance in application programming. Another consideration is that a large company usually has ongoing training programs into which it can easily fit a few more students at negligible additional expense to itself, whereas a small company may be unable to provide extensive training. If the small company does offer an initial training program, it may not be able to repeat it as staff replacements necessitate training new people. The vendor's future interest and ability to respond to problems are very important parts of a user's evaluation.

Actual installation should be preceded by careful planning and scheduling to guard against unforeseen difficulties. One precaution is to continue with the old way of doing the job until the new system is actually debugged and working.

Another aspect of installation that should not be overlooked is the type of training provided by the vendor. Although most training can be conducted by the vendor on his own premises, he should also arrange for on-site instruction as part of the installation procedure. Training should be detailed and supported by first-rate manuals covering both hardware and software. Well-organized, well-written documentation is also vital if the user's computer is to operate at its full potential.

SUMMARY

All factors discussed in this chapter should ideally be reducible to a single measure of a minicomputer's actual worth—its price/performance or value-per-dollar. Comparison of the price/performance figures of the minicomputers under consideration will then indicate which is the best buy. However simply that goal may be stated, its realization is far from simple. A given minicomputer may well be a "best buy" in terms of a particular application and the specific needs of an individual user, but there certainly is no "best" minicomputer. The only machines that can be rated as "best" are those better matched to some applications than to others, and perhaps lower priced than machines with comparable performance. The chief difficulty lies in defining the precision of that match, a difficulty compounded by the fact that part of the evaluation (the manufacturer's qualifications, for example) must be qualitative. In theory, the relative importance of each factor—machine parameters, available software, manufacturer's qualifications, and so on—could be numerically specified and a weighted score derived by totaling the contribution of each factor. The problem lies in the diversity of the potential applications and the resultant broad range in the weight to be assigned to each factor. The potential user must do his homework in specifying his application, using the kind of analysis presented in this chapter. This procedure should allow him to estimate the merits of one computer relative to other computers. Appendix A presents a comparison of the technical specifications of most minicomputers on the market today.

7. THE FUTURE OF MINICOMPUTERS

The minicomputer and the minicomputer industry are relatively new. As with most new industries and products, changes in the field have been rapid. These changes have resulted from advancing technology, a developing marketplace, competitive pressures among numerous suppliers, and external economic conditions. The continued impact of these factors will result in further evolution of the industry.

While the primary intent of this book is not to present a forecast for the minicomputer industry, it is appropriate that this chapter should conclude the book with a brief review of anticipated developments. Users must understand the pressures impacting the industry and the changes they are likely to effect, since these influences will reshape the industry and affect the viability of suppliers. Users who are looking for more than a solution to an immediate problem should estimate the effect of the changes on their suppliers. In the long run, the supplier's continued success is needed to assure an expanded line of peripherals and software for the user's minicomputer installation.

PRODUCTS AND TECHNOLOGY

Significant trends are apparent in minicomputer development. These trends relate to the complexity of minicomputers, prices, system architecture, and manufacturer's capabilities.

The Minicomputer as a Standard Component

The minicomputer mainframe is expected to become a commodity product. This will occur because the manufacturing process is primarily one of assembly, and the increased growth of MSI/LSI technology will substantially reduce the assembly operations required. The nature of the MSI/LSI manufacturing process should also increase standardization of minicomputer components. The manufacturing process requires extensive initial design of circuit partitions (assignment of functions to chips), device locations, masks, and interconnections. These fixed costs are a significant portion of the per-circuit cost. Therefore, the lowest per-circuit cost will be achieved by large production runs of standardized components. Semiconductor technology trends should also lead to a concentration of the manufacturing capacity of minicomputer components in the relatively few firms that obtain the largest production runs and lowest unit costs.

Minicomputer systems and traditional general-purpose computer systems are expected to continue their merging trends so that the point of demarcation between them will eventually disappear entirely. Minicomputer systems will be the low end on a continuous spectrum of computer products, and cost will become more difficult to use as a criterion in defining minicomputers. Memory size, cycle time, and other frequently used performance measurements are even now being discarded as guidelines in distinguishing minicomputers from large general-purpose systems.

Central Processor Prices

By the end of 1975, the cost-per-circuit function or cost-per-bit of memory is expected to decline by a factor of 5 to 10 under current prices. As a result of the lower circuit costs and reduced labor in component assembly, manufacturing costs of central processors should decline to approximately 40 percent of current values, and minicomputer central processors with 4000 bytes of memory should become available for approximately $1000 by 1975.

MINICOMPUTER ARCHITECTURE

The emergence of semiconductor memories will cause important changes in minicomputer architecture. Currently, semiconductor memories are less expensive (and faster) than core memories for sizes under 10,000 bits, or approximately 1000 bytes. The breakeven point will move upward and semiconductor memories will make inroads on core memory for the smaller memories associated with minicomputers. Semiconductor main memories yield faster machines but require new internal designs that use more parallelism to take advantage of the available memory speed. Read-only memories (ROM) are being used extensively. These will continue to be used for small high-speed memories used for storing microprograms and scratchpads, and for implementing special functions (firmware) such as table lookups or pushdown stacks that are otherwise implemented by software.

Reduction in semiconductor prices will lead to increased use of general-purpose hardware registers. These will be used as accumulators, index registers, pushdown stack pointers, and temporary storage to improve system performance.

Microprogrammed machines are now prevalent and should become even more so. The control logic in a conventional computer is unique to each computer and consists of an irregular assembly of specially designed circuit functions, which do not easily lend themselves to MSI/LSI. In a microprogrammed machine the control logic is embedded in a high-speed memory that reduces the amount of random logic in a processor and allows greater use of MSI/LSI. This approach allows high-volume production of nearly identical processors, which can be tuned to a specific application by including a selected instruction set in the microprogram memory. The microprogrammed approach also provides flexibility to use existing software developed for earlier machines, thus reducing future software development costs.

Need for Semiconductor Expertise

The changes occurring in semiconductor technology will require increased expertise from the minicomputer manufacturers. The objective of system design will change to optimizing circuit densities as well as the interconnections between MSI/LSI arrays as opposed to minimizing circuit counts for discrete components and low-density ICs. With a drop in the number of logic packages in the minicomputer, the partitioning of functions into these packages is critical. Thus, optimal machine designs and production will require extensive knowledge of semiconductors by the manufacturer.

THE MARKETPLACE

Computer industry analysts concur in their projections for continued growth in the use of minicomputers. The potential applications for these machines are enormous. Eventually, these machines or their descendants are likely to penetrate almost every aspect of industrial and consumer activities.

The single, most important factor that will limit the growth of minicomputer applications is the ability of users to absorb the systems offered. Several basic resources, including money and personnel, are necessary to apply a minicomputer. Among the important factors that will control the rate of growth of minicomputers are:

National economy: If the national economy remains stable, the minicomputer industry should thrive.

System cost: Although minicomputer mainframe prices are relatively low and are declining, total system cost is extensive when peripherals, system design, and programming are all considered. Furthermore, the anticipated declines in minicomputer prices will not necessarily open new markets because total system costs, which include all other equipment and personnel, will not decline at the same rate as mainframes.

Availability of personnel: Successful application of a minicomputer requires knowledge of the minicomputer capability to perform a required function, system design, program design, and program implementation, all of which require trained personnel.

Computer justification: Application of a minicomputer requires feasibility analysis and justification, which can be time-consuming and may serve as a constraining influence.

User acceptance: Potential users must learn that minicomputers are reasonable alternatives for their applications; this occurs gradually in a new market area.

Considering these factors, most analysts agree that minicomputer sales will grow by 15 to 25 percent a year for the next few years, spurred by a steady decline in the price of an average system and a growing awareness of these systems.

APPENDIX A:
MINICOMPUTER COMPARISON CHARTS

INTRODUCTION

These charts summarize the mainframe characteristics of 89 minicomputers on the market today. Systems are listed in alphabetical order by manufacturer. Each chart is divided into five sections: Data Structure, Central Processor, Working Storage, Read-Only Memory, and General Features and Comments. The last section provides any necessary amplification of the information in the rest of the chart; it is reserved for short notes on any important features of the machines that are peculiar to the system under consideration or are not adequately presented in the tabular entries. Detailed descriptions of each entry in the other four sections follow.

DATA STRUCTURE

System Identity.   Manufacturer's designation for the minicomputer system.

Word Length.   Number of bits in one computer word. Some minicomputer words include parity or memory protection bits, which do not contribute to the word's data capacity; in such cases, the entry is of the form x + y, where "x" is the number of data bits and "y" is the number of nondata bits in each word.

Sometimes there is ambiguity about the exact definition of word length because the core storage capacity and access time may be given in terms of bytes or half-words.

The figure given in this entry corresponds to the use of the term "word" by the mainframe manufacturer and is not necessarily the same as the number of bits in the smallest physical division of working storage.

Operand Length.   Specifies the number of bits accessible by a single hardware instruction. An asterisk means that the operands are accessible only by instructions provided with an optional hardware feature.

The entry may include more than one decimal number, starting with the smallest operand size; for a complex system, operand size may range from one bit (denoting the availability of single-bit manipulation instructions) to the number of bits in floating-point or double-length numbers (denoting the presence of hardware facilities for manipulating these entities).

Instruction Length.   Different instruction lengths are given, starting with the smallest. Some minicomputers use two instruction lengths, one for instructions that do not address main memory and the other for instructions that do address main memory.

Floating-Point Format.   The number of bits in the fraction and exponent are given for the standard floating-point format(s).

CENTRAL PROCESSOR

Model Number.   Manufacturer's identifying number for the processor.

Number of Instructions.   Number of different instructions in the standard basic instruction set for the processor. Some minicomputers combine a number of operations in one instruction by a technique sometimes called "microprogramming," which allows different bit settings to specify different operations; for such computers, only the number of different basic instructions is given, and the extra permissible microprogrammed combinations are not included.

Address Bits—Memory.   Largest number of bits available to address a main memory location in any instruction. If the whole of main memory is addressable from an instruction, this number will correspond to the largest main memory capacity; for example, 14 bits for a maximum memory of 32,768 (2^{15} words).

Usually, the main memory is conceptually divided into "pages," and only locations in certain pages are directly addressable from an instruction; for example, there may be seven address bits, corresponding to 256 (2^8) addressable locations in each page. In such cases, the format for memory reference instructions frequently includes flag bits to specify the page being addressed (such as current page/base page); these flag bits are not included in the number given in the chart.

Address Bits—Devices.   Number of bits available in an input/output instruction or control word to specify an input/output device number. This indicates the number of different devices the processor can address.

Indirect Addressing.   Availability and number of levels of indirect addressing. An indirect address specifies a storage location that contains either a direct address (that is, the address of an operand) or another indirect address.

Number of General-Purpose Registers.   Number of registers available to hold operands or results for instructions. A double-length accumulator counts as two registers only if the two halves of it are separately addressable.

Note that some of the general-purpose registers may also be used as index registers and counted in the entry for the number of index registers.

Number of Index Registers.   Number of special registers provided to hold indexers that can be added to the address portion of an instruction prior to its execution. Indexing and indirect addressing are the principal techniques used for address modification and can greatly simplify programming.

Note that some of or all index registers may also be counted in the entry for the number of general-purpose registers.

Interrupt Lines and Levels.   Program interrupt is a hardware facility that initiates the execution of a different sequence of instructions upon request when a specific internal or external signal occurs. Software routines can simulate any required interrupt system, using one interrupt line. Most computers, however, provide something in addition to a minimum interrupt system. Computer manufacturers describe more complex interrupt systems in terms of interrupt lines and interrupt levels, but not all manufacturers use these terms in the same way.

To clarify the distinction between interrupt lines and interrupt levels, the following discussion defines both for the purpose of these comparison charts.

An *interrupt line* automatically generates the address of a core location that contains the initial address of the interrupt servicing subroutine. Some systems enter the servicing subroutine by generating an EXECUTE instruction, with the address field supplied by a particular interrupt line. Other systems generate a JUMP indirect instruction with the address field supplied by a particular interrupt line. The former method is efficient if an interrupt servicing routine can consist of only one instruction. On the other hand, this method requires the execution of one additional instruction (the EXECUTE) before entering the interrupt servicing routine if it consists of two or more instructions. This second method is efficient in systems where interrupt servicing routines always consist of two or more instructions.

An *interrupt level* represents a priority distinction within an interrupt system. Some priority interrupt systems consist of a number of interrupt levels that are multiplexed into a smaller number of interrupt lines or even one line. In other systems, each interrupt line has only one interrupt level. In still other systems some interrupt lines have only one interrupt level, while other lines are subdivided into a number of interrupt levels.

Standard Interrupt Problem I.   Time in microseconds is given for the execution of Standard Interrupt Problem I, which measures the time for software activities necessary to service an interrupt. This is an important factor in the selection of a minicomputer for real-time applications.

Standard Interrupt Problem I gives the time for storing all processor registers at the beginning of an interrupt servicing sequence and for restoring them again at the end of the sequence; it also includes the time required to disable and enable other interrupts. The time given does not include the execution time of the servicing routine itself.

Standard Interrupt Problem II.   Time in microseconds required to determine which device on a given interrupt line caused an interrupt. The time is zero if each device selects a unique core location for entry to the interrupt servicing routine; otherwise, the time is an essential part of the interrupt system's response time and must be added to the time given for Standard Interrupt Problem I when evaluating the real-time capabilities of a given minicomputer.

Fixed-Point Execute Time.   Number of microseconds normally required to perform addition (c = a + b), multiplication (c = ab), and division (c = a/b), using operands expressed in the standard fixed-point representation listed under "Data Structure" in the charts. All listed execution times include the time required to access both operands from and to store the result in working storage.

Floating-Point Execute Time.   Number of microseconds normally required to perform addition (c = a + b), multiplication (c = ab), and division (c = a/b), using operands expressed in the standard floating-point representation listed in the charts under "Data Structure." All listed execution times include the time required to access both operands from and to store the result in working storage.

Real-Time Clock.   Availability of a real-time clock feature for the processor. This may be standard, optional, or unavailable. Real-time clocks indicate the passage of time, to the processor, independent of the particular instructions executed; physically, an interrupt level is associated with the clock. This feature is necessary for many minicomputer control applications.

Input/Output Channels.   Input/output channels for the processor are described briefly. Normally, there is a programmed input/output bus (PIO) available to a number of peripheral devices; a common option is a direct memory access (DMA) facility providing communication between fast external devices and main memory on a cycle-stealing basis.

WORKING STORAGE

Model Number.   Manufacturer's identifying number.

Type of Storage.   Storage medium used in this unit, usually ferrite cores but occasionally thin-film or integrated circuits.

Number of Words.   Minimum and maximum working storage capacity, expressed in terms of the word length specified under "Data Structure" in the charts.

Cycle Time.   Minimum time interval, in microseconds, between two successive accesses to a particular storage location.

Bits per Cycle.   Number of bits of information transferred to or from the working storage each time it is accessed. Usually, but not invariably, this quantity will be the same as the number of data bits in one word.

Parity.   Availability of a parity checking feature for the working storage.

Memory Protect.   Availability of a feature for the selective protection of designated areas of main memory from reading, or overwriting, or both.

READ-ONLY MEMORY

Availability.   Read-only memory (ROM) for a particular minicomputer system may be unavailable, available as an option, or included as a standard feature.

Use.   For a given minicomputer system, ROM may be used in one or more ways: to hold microinstructions to define the instruction set of the machine as it appears to the programmer, to hold parts of the standard software, or to hold standard user programs that will not be altered. This entry briefly gives the use of ROM for the particular computer system.

SPECIFICATION CHARTS
Processors and Working Storage

	SYSTEM IDENTITY		Cincinnati Milacron CIP/2100	Cincinnati Milacron CIP/2200	Computer Automation Alpha 8	Computer Automation Alpha 16	Computer Signal Processors CSP-30
DATA STRUCTURE	Word Length, bits		8	8	8	16	16
	Operand Lengths, bits		8	8	8	8; 16	16
	Inst Lengths, bits		16	16	8; 16	16	16; 32
	Floating Point Format	Fract, bits	NA	NA	NA	23 + sign	24 + sign
		Exp, bits	NA	NA	NA	7 + sign	7
CENTRAL PROCESSOR	Model Number		CIP/2000	CIP/2000	Alpha 8	Alpha 16	CSP-30
	No. of Instructions		88[1]	119[1]	76	144	291
	Address Bits	Memory	8	8	8	8	8; 10
		Devices	8	8	8	8	NA
	Indirect Addressing		1 level	1 level	Multilevel	Multilevel	Multilevel
	No. G P Reg		2	2	1	2	32
	No. Index Reg		1	1	None	1	15
	Interrupt	Lines	8	8	3-72*	2-66*	1
		Levels	1-64	1-64	3-72*	No limit	7 std; increments of 6 opt
	Interrupt Response Times, μsec	SIP I	72.9	72.9	47.2	37.6	NA
		SIP II	7.04-13.2	7.04-13.2	0.0	0.0	NA
	Fixed-Point Execute Time, μsec	c=a+b	35.0	35.0	20.8	12.8	1.2 (IC)
		c=ab	93.3	93.3	180.(s)	34.0	2.1 (IC)
		c=a/b	120.8	120.8	370.(s)	38.0	4.9 (IC)
	Floating-Point Execute Time, μsec	c=a+b	NA	NA	NA	NA	NA
		c=ab	NA	NA	NA	NA	NA
		c=a/b	NA	NA	NA	NA	NA
	Real-Time Clock		Yes*	Yes*	Yes*	Yes*	NA
	Input/Output Channels		DMA; concurrent parallel I/O	DMA; concurrent parallel I/O	I/O bus	I/O bus; DMA*	Up to 4 party lines; dual-port DMA
WORKING STORAGE	Model Number		CIP/2000	CIP/2000	11211	11211	CSP-30
	Type of Storage		Ferrite core	Ferrite core	Magnetic core	Magnetic core	Magnetic core/IC
	Number of Words	Min	4,096	4,096	4,096	2,048	8,192/512
		Max	32,768	32,768	32,768	32,768	131,072/2,048
	Cycle Time, μsec		1.1	1.1	1.6	1.6	0.9; 0.1
	Bits per Cycle		8	8	8	16	16
	Parity		Yes*	Yes*	Yes*	Yes*	No
	Memory Protect		Yes*	Yes*	Yes*	Yes*	No
ROM	Availability		4K-32K words	4K to 32K words	512-8,192 words*	256-4,096 words*	None
	Use		Program	Program	Defines program	Defines program	—
	General Features and Comments		(1) Decimal arithmetic; memory-to-memory instructions	(1) Decimal arithmetic; memory-to-memory instructions	Upward software and I/O compatible with other CA 8-bit computers; Naked Mini 8 version available without power supply and console	Upward software and I/O compatible with other CA 16-bit computers; Naked Mini 16 version available without power supply and console	Magnetic core and fast integrated circuit memory are intermixed on a system; both can store either programs or data; memory modules can have up to 8 ports of entry

* With optional equipment
(s)Using subroutine
N Number of devices tested

SYSTEM IDENTITY	Control Data CDC 1704	Control Data CDC SC 1700	Control Data CDC 1714	Data General Nova[1]	Data General Nova 800/820[1]
DATA STRUCTURE					
Word Length, bits	16 data; 1 parity; 1 protect	16 data; 1 parity; 1 protect	16 data; 1 parity; 1 protect	16	16
Operand Lengths, bits	16	16	16	16	16
Inst Lengths, bits	16	16	16	16	16
Floating Point Format — Fract, bits	23 + sign	23 + sign	23 + sign	24 or 56 + sign	24 or 56 + sign
Floating Point Format — Exp, bits	8	8	8	7	7
CENTRAL PROCESSOR					
Model Number	1704	1774	1714	4001	Nova 800/820
No. of Instructions	74	74	74	202	202
Address Bits — Memory	8; 15 (indirect)	8; 15 (indirect)	8; 15; 16 (indirect)[1]	8	8
Address Bits — Devices	9	9	9	6	6
Indirect Addressing	Multilevel	Multilevel	1 level[1]	Multilevel	Multilevel
No. G P Reg	1	1	1	4	4
No. Index Reg	2[1]	2[1]	2[2]	2	2
Interrupt — Lines	2; 16*	2; 16*	2; 16*	1	1
Interrupt — Levels	16	16	16	16	16
Interrupt Response Times, μsec — SIP I	29.7	41.0	29.7	130.7	43.7
Interrupt Response Times, μsec — SIP II	5.5	8.5	5.5	9.9	3.8
Fixed-Point Execute Time, μsec — c=a+b	6.6	9.0	6.6	29.6	8.0
Fixed-Point Execute Time, μsec — c=ab	11.4	15.5	11.4	101*	30*
Fixed-Point Execute Time, μsec — c=a/b	15.8	21.5	15.8	167*	46*
Floating-Point Execute Time, μsec — c=a+b	16.5(s)	225 (s)	165 (s)	50.4*	20.0*
Floating-Point Execute Time, μsec — c=ab	265 (s)	361 (s)	265 (s)	53.5*	23.7*
Floating-Point Execute Time, μsec — c=a/b	465 (s)	634 (s)	465 (s)	56.3*	26.5*
Real-Time Clock	No	No	No	Yes*	Yes*
Input/Output Channels	Integrated[2], I/O bus; up to 3 DSA and/or buffered	Integrated[2], I/O bus; up to 3 DSA and/or buffered	Integrated[3], I/O bus; up to 3 DSA and/or buffered	Programmed I/O bus; DMA	Programmed I/O bus; DMA, high-speed data channel
WORKING STORAGE					
Model Number	CDC 1704	CDC SC1700	CDC 1714	4003/4/8016	8203/04/15/16; 8271/2/3/4
Type of Storage	Magnetic core	Magnetic core	Magnetic core	Magnetic core	Magnetic core
Number of Words — Min	4,096	4,096	24,576	2,048	1,024
Number of Words — Max	32,768	32,768	65,536[4]	32,768	32,768; 65K[2]
Cycle Time, μsec	1.1	1.5	1.1	2.6	0.8
Bits per Cycle	16 data; 1 parity; 1 protect	16 data; 1 parity; 1 protect	16 data; 1 parity; 1 protect	16	16
Parity	Std	Std	Std	No	No
Memory Protect	Std	Std	Std	No	No
ROM					
Availability	None	None	None	256 to max memory	256 to max memory
Use	--	—	—	Program protection	Program protection
General Features and Comments	(1) 1 index register in core (2) For console, paper tape reader/punch	(1) Both index registers are hardware registers (2) For console only	(1) Multilevel in 32K mode only (2) 1 core index register (3) For cnsle only; p. tape rdr/pnch by special order (4) Arranged in 2 dual port banks, allowing interleaved memory accesses	(1) Nova is no longer marketed (2) By floating-point interpreter	(1) Nova 820 uses an integrated back-panel power supply that eliminates 1 Nova 800 subsystem (2) Not software supported

* With optional equipment
(s) Using subroutine
N Number of devices tested

	SYSTEM IDENTITY		Data General Nova 840[1]	Data General Nova 1200/1210/1220[1]	Data General Supernova and SC[1]	Datacraft DC-6024/1	Datacraft DC-6024/3
DATA STRUCTURE	Word Length, bits		16	16	16	24 + parity	24 + parity
	Operand Lengths, bits		16	16	16	24; 16; 8	24; 16; 8
	Inst Lengths, bits		16	16	16	24	24
	Floating Point Format	Fract, bits	24 or 56 + sign	24 or 56 + sign	24 or 56 + sign	23 or 38 + sign	23 or 38 + sign
		Exp, bits	7	7	7	7 + sign	7 + sign
CENTRAL PROCESSOR	Model Number		8202	Nova 1200/1210/1220	8001	DC-6024/1	DC-6024/3
	No. of Instructions		202	202	202	596	584
	Address Bits	Memory	8	8	8	15	15
		Devices	6	6	6	9	9
	Indirect Addressing		Multilevel	Multilevel	Multilevel	Multilevel	Multilevel
	No. G P Reg		4	4	4	5	5
	No. Index Reg		2	2	2	3	3
	Interrupt	Lines	1	1	1	4; 68*	4; 20*
		Levels	16	16	16	80	32
	Interrupt Response Times, μsec	SIP I	43.7	63.8	47.3/48.6	6.6	11.2
		SIP II	3.8	5.1	5.3/4.8	4.8	8.2
	Fixed-Point Execute Time, μsec	c=a+b	8.0	12.6	8.0/5.7	5.4	9.2
		c=ab	25*	36.0*	25*/19.1*	8.4	14.3
		c=a/b	44.1*	60.3*	46*/22.6	12.6	21.4
	Floating-Point Execute Time, μsec	c=a+b	20.0*	25.65*	21.9*	7.2	12.0
		c=ab	23.7*	28.75*	25.0*	10.2	17.0
		c=a/b	26.5*	31.55*	27.8*	13.8	21.4
	Real-Time Clock		Optional	Optional	Optional	Optional	Optional
	Input/Output Channels		Programmed I/O bus; DMA; high-speed data channel	Programmed I/O bus; DMA; high-speed data channel	Programmed I/O bus; DMA, high-speed data channel	Up to 28 programmed I/O; (8 or 24 bits wide); ABC (DMA) opt	Up to 14 programmed I/O; (8 or 24 bits wide); ABC (DMA) opt
WORKING STORAGE	Model Number		8203, 04, 15, 16[2]	8103/04/15/16; 8171/2/3/4	8003/15; 8012/13/14	DC-6024/1	DC-6024/3
	Type of Storage		Core	Magnetic core	Core/semiconductor	Magnetic core	Magnetic core
	Number of Words	Min	1,024	1,024	4K/256	8,192	8,192
		Max	131,072	32,768; 65K[2]	32,768; 65K[2]	65,536	65,536
	Cycle Time, μsec		0.8	1.2	0.8; 0.3	0.6	1.0
	Bits per Cycle		16	16	16	24 + parity	24 + parity
	Parity		No	No	No	Std	Std
	Memory Protect		Option	Option	Option	Optional	Optional
ROM	Availability		256 to max memory	256 to max memory	256 to max memory	None	None
	Use		Program protection	Program protection	Program protection	—	—
	General Features and Comments		(1) Previously called Nova 800 Jumbo; 15 subassembly slots in chassis; only processor that supports memory management option (2) 1K, 2K, 4K, or 8K increments	(1) Nova 1210 and 1220 use an integrated power supply that eliminates 1 Nova 1200 subsystem Nova 1210, 1220 differ in no. of circuit board slots (2) Not software supported	(1) Supernova and Supernova SC use the same processor, differ only in memory used; Supernova uses core, Supernova SC uses SC memory (2) Not software supported	Floating-point operations are performed by external Scientific Arithmetic Unit (SAU) or by subroutine; opt bit processor	Same as DC-6024/1

* With optional equipment
(s)Using subroutine
N Number of devices tested

	SYSTEM IDENTITY	Datacraft 6024/4	Datacraft DC-6024/5, 5R[1]	Datamate Computer DM-16	Datamate Computer DM-70	DCC D-112[1]
DATA STRUCTURE	Word Length, bits	24 + 1 parity	24 + parity	16	16	12
	Operand Lengths, bits	24	24; 16; 8	8; 16; 32	8; 16; 32	12
	Inst Lengths, bits	23	24	16	16	12
	Floating Point Format — Fract, bits	23 or 38 + sign	23 or 38 + sign	23 or 54 + sign	NA	23 + sign
	Floating Point Format — Exp, bits	7 + sign	7 + sign	8	NA	11 + sign
CENTRAL PROCESSOR	Model Number	6024/4	DC-6024/5	DM-16	DM-70	D-112
	No. of Instructions	584	592	Over 80	Over 144	28 std; 12 opt
	Address Bits — Memory	15	15	8	9	7
	Address Bits — Devices	9	9	6	6	6
	Indirect Addressing	Multilevel	Multilevel	Multilevel	Multilevel	1 level
	No. G P Reg	5	5	1	4	1 + extension
	No. Index Reg	3	3	1	2	0 (8 auto index)
	Interrupt — Lines	4; 20*	4; 20*	8–64*	1–64*	1
	Interrupt — Levels	64	32	64	64	1
	Interrupt Response Times, μsec — SIP I	4.5	6.0	4.0	7.0	34.8
	Interrupt Response Times, μsec — SIP II	2.25	3.0	0	0	5.8N[2]
	Fixed-Point Execute Time, μsec — c=a+b	4.5	6.0	6.0	6.0	12.0
	Fixed-Point Execute Time, μsec — c=ab	9.0	12.0	11.0	11.0	32.6*
	Fixed-Point Execute Time, μsec — c=a/b	14.3	19.0	13.0	13.0	45.4*
	Floating-Point Execute Time, μsec — c=a+b	9.0	33 (s)	124 (s)	NA	387 (s)
	Floating-Point Execute Time, μsec — c=ab	12.8	28 (s)	191 (s)	NA	467 (s)*
	Floating-Point Execute Time, μsec — c=a/b	16.1	34 (s)	177 (s)	NA	511 (s)*
	Real-Time Clock	Opt	Yes*	Yes*	Yes*	Yes*
	Input/Output Channels	Up to 48 programmed I/O (8 or 24-bits wide); up to 12 ABC (DMA) opt	Up to 24 programmed I/O; (8 or 24-bits wide); ABC (DMA) opt	Programmed I/O bus; DMA	Programmed I/O bus; DMA	Programmed I/O; Data Break*
WORKING STORAGE	Model Number	402/402	DC-6024/5	DM-16	DM-70	MM-1
	Type of Storage	Core/SC[1]	Magnetic core	Magnetic core	Magnetic core[1]	Core
	Number of Words — Min	8K	4,096	4,096	4,096[1]	256/4K
	Number of Words — Max	256K[2]/16K[3]	65,536	32,768	32,768	32K
	Cycle Time, μsec	0.75/0.20	1.0	1.0	1.0, 0.8[1]	1.2
	Bits per Cycle	24 + 1 parity	24 + parity	16	16	12
	Parity	Std	Std	No	No	Opt
	Memory Protect	Opt	Opt	No	No	No
ROM	Availability	None	None	None	Yes[2]	Yes
	Use	—	—	—	Interchangeable with core	Program
	General Features and Comments	(1) SC memory has 2 ports of entry (2) With virtual memory addressing (3) Requires I/O processor for dual port	Floating-point hardware unavailable (1) Ruggedized version	Designed for data acquisition, manipulation, logging and analysis applications, and for process and instrument control	(1) Semiconductor read/write memory available in 64-word modules (2) ROM available in 256-word modules	(1) DCC claims the D-122 is program-compatible with PDP-8/I, PDP-8/L, and PDP-8/E

* With optional equipment
(s)Using subroutine
N Number of devices tested

		DCC D112-H and D-112 H/SC	DCC D-116[1]	Digital Equipment PDP-8/E/M/F[1]	Digital Equipment PDP-11/05/10[1]	Digital Equipment PDP-11/15/20
DATA STRUCTURE	**SYSTEM IDENTITY**					
	Word Length, bits	12	16	12	16	16
	Operand Lengths, bits	12	16	12	1; 8; 16	1; 8; 16
	Inst Lengths, bits	12	16	12	16; 32; 48	16; 32; 48
	Floating Point Format — Fract, bits	23 + sign	24 + sign	23 + sign	23 or 55 + sign	23 or 55 + sign
	Floating Point Format — Exp, bits	11 + sign	7	11 + sign	8	8
CENTRAL PROCESSOR	Model Number	D-112H; D-112H/SC	D116	PDP-8/E/M/F	KD11-B	KC11/KA11
	No. of Instructions	37 std, 13 opt	19 std, 2 opt	56 + 16*	75[2]	75[1]
	Address Bits — Memory	7	8	8	6[3]	6[2]
	Address Bits — Devices	6	6	6	6	6
	Indirect Addressing	1 level	Multilevel	1 level	1 level	1 level
	No. G P Reg	1 +	4	1 + extension	6	6
	No. Index Reg	0 (8 auto index + 16*)	2	0 (15 auto index in core)	8	6
	Interrupt — Lines	1	1	1	1 int; 1 ext	1 int; 4 ext[3]
	Interrupt — Levels	1	16	1	1 int; 1 ext	5 int; 4 ext[3]
	Interrupt Response Times, μsec — SIP I	26.1/8.7	63.8	34.8	12.0	12.0
	Interrupt Response Times, μsec — SIP II	4.4N/1.6N	5.1	5.8N	0	0
	Fixed-Point Execute Time, μsec — c=a+b	8.1/2.7	12.6	12.0	22.7	18.8
	Fixed-Point Execute Time, μsec — c=ab	12.6*/6.0*	36.0*	32.6 (EAE opt)	43.5	36.7[1]
	Fixed-Point Execute Time, μsec — c=a/b	12.6*/6.0*	60.3*	45.4 (EAE opt)	43.8	37.0[1]
	Floating-Point Execute Time, μsec — c=a+b	290 (s)/97 (s)	270	387 (s)	376 (s)	314 (s)
	Floating-Point Execute Time, μsec — c=ab	350 (s)*/123.6 (s)*	655	467 (s, EAE opt)	1017 (s)	848 (s)
	Floating-Point Execute Time, μsec — c=a/b	383 (s)/194.2 (s)*	730	511 (s, EAE opt)	2169 (s)	1,808 (s)
	Real-Time Clock	Yes*	Yes*	Yes*	Yes*	Yes*
	Input/Output Channels	Programmed I/O; Data Break*	Programmed I/O; DMA	Programmed I/O; up to 12 data break (DMA)	UNIBUS (programmed I/O and DMA)	UNIBUS (programmed I/O and DMA)
WORKING STORAGE	Model Number	MM-1/MC-1	D-116	MM8-E	MM11	MM11
	Type of Storage	Core/SC	Core	Magnetic core	Magnetic core	Magnetic core
	Number of Words — Min	4K/256	2K	256/4,096	1K/2K/4K/8K[4]	1K/2K/4K/8K[4]
	Number of Words — Max	32K/8K	32K	32,768	28,672	28,672
	Cycle Time, μsec	0.9; 0.3[2]	1.2	1.2	1.2; 0.95; 0.9	1.2; 0.95; 0.9
	Bits per Cycle	12	16	12	16	16
	Parity	Opt	No	Opt	No[5]	No[5]
	Memory Protect	No	No	No	No	No
ROM	Availability	Yes	Yes	256/1K words	32/1K words	32/1K words
	Use	Program	Program	Program protection	Bootstrap loaders; program protection	Bootstrap loaders; program protection
	General Features and Comments	(1) DCC claims D-122H/SC is program and peripheral compatible with the PDP-8 Series (2) Max; 0.2 min	(1) DCC claims the D-116 is plug- and program-compatible with the Nova 1200 Series	(1) Upward compatible with earlier PDP-8 models; PDP-8/M & F are physically smaller than PDP-8/E; can be upgraded to PDP-8/E	(1) 3 and 5 for OEM 10 for end users (2) EAE option is I/O device (3) All addresses select index register (4) Memories can be intermixed on a system (5) Special order	(1) EAE option is I/O device for hardware x, ÷ (2) All addresses select index register (3) 1 line std on KC11 (4) 8K modules are interleaved 4K modules (5) Special order

* With optional equipment
(s) Using subroutine
N Number of devices tested

	SYSTEM IDENTITY	Digital Equipment PDP-11/40	Digital Equipment PDP-11/45	Digital Equipment PDP-11/45	Digital Equipment PDP-11/50	Digital Equipment PDP-12
DATA STRUCTURE	Word Length, bits	16	16 + 2*	16 + 2*	16 + 2*	12
	Operand Lengths, bits	8; 16	1; 8; 16; 32	1; 8; 16; 32	1; 8; 16; 32	12
	Inst Lengths, bits	16; 32; 48	16; 32; 48	16; 32; 48	16; 32; 48	12
	Floating Point Format — Fract, bits	23 + sign	23 or 55 + sign	23 or 55 + sign	23 or 55 + sign	23 + sign
	Floating Point Format — Exp, bits	8 (in excess 128)	8	8	8	8
CENTRAL PROCESSOR	Model Number	—	KB11	KB11	KB11	10/20/30/40/LPD/TSS
	No. of Instructions	55 std + 8 opt	128[1]	128[1]	128[1]	56 + 12[1] + 34
	Address Bits — Memory	16	6	6[2]	6[2]	8/10
	Address Bits — Devices	16	6	6	6	6
	Indirect Addressing	1 level	1 level	1 level	1 level	1 level
	No. G P Reg	8 + 1[1]	6 (2 sets)	6 (2 sets)	6 (2 sets)	1
	No. Index Reg	8 + 1[1]	6 (2 sets)	6 (2 sets)	6 (2 sets)	0 (auto-index registers in core)
	Interrupt — Lines	4	4 int; 4 ext	4 int; 4 ext	4 int; 4 ext	1
	Interrupt — Levels	Multilevel	20[3]	20[3]	20[3]	1
	Interrupt Response Times, μsec — SIP I	41.08[2]	4.1	4.1	4.1	45.2
	Interrupt Response Times, μsec — SIP II	5.42	0	0	0	7.5N
	Fixed-Point Execute Time, μsec — c=a+b	11.58	7.8	3.8	5.0	10.9
	Fixed-Point Execute Time, μsec — c=ab	16.98	10.5	6.5	7.7	42.4
	Fixed-Point Execute Time, μsec — c=a/b	20.39	14.3	10.5	11.5	59.0[1]
	Floating-Point Execute Time, μsec — c=a+b	48.30[3]	14.5	8.8	9.8	503.1[2]
	Floating-Point Execute Time, μsec — c=ab	58.52	16.3	10.4	11.6	607.1[2]
	Floating-Point Execute Time, μsec — c=a/b	76.24	21.0	14.7	16.3	664.3[2]
	Real-Time Clock	Yes*	Yes*	Yes*	Yes*	Yes
	Input/Output Channels	INFIBUS, PIO, and DMA inherent	UNIBUS (programmed I/O and DMA)	UNIBUS; separate bus to bipolar memory	UNIBUS; separate bus to MOS memory	Programmed I/O and data break (1 and 3-cycle)
WORKING STORAGE	Model Number	MM11-S, MF11-L, ML11(4)	MM11[4]	MS11-C[4]	MS11-B[4]	MC12/MM81
	Type of Storage	Core	Magnetic core	Bipolar	MOS	Core memory
	Number of Words — Min	1K	4K/8K	4,096	4,096	4,096
	Number of Words — Max	128K	126,976	8,192	32,768	32,768
	Cycle Time, μsec	0.9	0.88	0.350	0.450	1.6
	Bits per Cycle	16	16	16	16	12
	Parity	Special order	Opt; 1 bit/byte	Opt	Opt	Opt
	Memory Protect	Opt	Yes	Opt	Opt	Opt
ROM	Availability	Yes	32/1K words	32/1K words	32/1K words	No
	Use	Loaders; program	Bootstrap loaders; program protection	Program loaders; program protection	Program loaders; program protection	—
	General Features and Comments	(1) With memory management option (2) Assumes all registers saved (3) Assumes exponents differ by no more than 1 (4) Memories can be mixed on a system	(1) Includes PDP-11 basic set, x, ÷, and single- and double-precision floating point (2) All addresses select index reg (3) 7 software levels (4) Memories can be intermixed on system	(1) Includes PDP-11 basic set, x, ÷, and single- and double-precision floating point (2) All addresses select index reg (3) 7 software levels (4) Memories can be intermixed on system	(1) Includes PDP-11 basic set, x, ÷, and single- and double-precision floating point (2) All addresses select index reg (3) 7 software levels (4) MOS memory can also be used on the 11/45	Includes PDP-8 basic instrctn set + LINC instrctn set (1) With EAE option (2) By subroutine; Models 40 and LDP include hardware floating-point processor

* With optional equipment
(s)Using subroutine
N Number of devices tested

	SYSTEM IDENTITY	Digital Equipment PDP-15/10 to /50	Digital Equipment PDP-15/70 Series	Digital Scientific META 4	Electronic Associates EAI PACER 100	Electronic Processors EPI-118/218
DATA STRUCTURE	Word Length, bits	18	18	16	16	18
	Operand Lengths, bits	18	18	16; 32	16; 32	3; 18*; 18
	Inst Lengths, bits	18	18	16	16	18
	Floating Point Format — Fract, bits	26 + sign	26 + sign	23 + sign	23 + sign	—
	Floating Point Format — Exp, bits	8 + sign	8 + sign	8	7 + sign	—
CENTRAL PROCESSOR	Model Number	KP15[1]	KP15[1]	META 4	1150	EPI-118/218
	No. of Instructions	110 + 29[2]	110 + 29[2]	44	64 + 9[1] + 6[2]	22 + 16*/192
	Address Bits — Memory	12	12	6; 15	9 or 8 + sign	9; 12; 15
	Address Bits — Devices	6	6	NA	6	6
	Indirect Addressing	1 level	1 level	1 level	Multilevel[3]	No; multilevel
	No. G P Reg	1	1	Up to 28	2	1 (3-bit), 1 (18-bit); 2 (18-bit)
	No. Index Reg	1 (+ auto-index registers in core)	1 (+ auto-index registers in core)	Up to 28	1 + core index	0; 3
	Interrupt — Lines	1	1	1	4	1
	Interrupt — Levels	32*	32*	Increments of 12	64	19
	Interrupt Response Times, μsec — SIP I	20.0	25.0	NA	0	12.5
	Interrupt Response Times, μsec — SIP II	2.8N; 0*	3.58N; 0*	NA	3.5	2.0[1]
	Fixed-Point Execute Time, μsec — c=a+b	4.8	6.0	8.2	6	4.0
	Fixed-Point Execute Time, μsec — c=ab	13.6[2]	14.8[2]	11.0	9.6	NA
	Fixed-Point Execute Time, μsec — c=a/b	17.0[2]	18.2[2]	14.2	10.6	NA
	Floating-Point Execute Time, μsec — c=a+b	227.2	232	14.8	11.4*[4]	(S)
	Floating-Point Execute Time, μsec — c=ab	208[2]	212[2]	22.8	19.4*[4]	(S)
	Floating-Point Execute Time, μsec — c=a/b	256[2]	260[2]	28.8	20.2*[4]	(S)
	Real-Time Clock	Yes	Yes	Yes	Yes	Yes
	Input/Output Channels	Programmed I/O and data break (1-and multicycle)	Programmed I/O and data break (1- and multicycle)	Programmed I/O; up to 9 DMA per memory port	4 programmed I/O; 2 DMA opt; drum channel opt	Programmed I/O; DMA*
WORKING STORAGE	Model Number	MM15	ME15	—	1180/1186	EPI-118/218
	Type of Storage	Core memory	Core memory	Magnetic core[1]	Core	Core memory
	Number of Words — Min	4,096	8,192	4,096	8K/16K	4,096
	Number of Words — Max	32,768/128K[3]	96K	65,536	32K	32,768
	Cycle Time, μsec	0.8	0.980	0.9	1.0	0.9; 0.96
	Bits per Cycle	18	18	16	16	18
	Parity	Opt	Opt	Yes	No	No
	Memory Protect	Opt	Opt	Yes	Yes	No
ROM	Availability	No	No	1K to 4K words	Std	No
	Use	—	—	Microprogramming	Bootstrap	—
	General Features and Comments	(1) PDP-15/50 includes the FP15 Floating-Point Processor; FP15 opt on other models (2) With EAE option (3) With MX15 memory multiplexer	(1) PDP-15/79 includes the FP15 Floating-Point Processor; FP15 opt on other models (2) With EAE	Designed as user-oriented controller or emulator; firmware available for emulation of IBM 1130, IBM 1800, and CDC 160A(1) Up to 256 words of IC scratchpad memory	(1) Double-precision integer (2) Optional floating point (3) Pre- and post-index indirect (4) Unnormalized hexadecimal floating point	(1) With priority interrupt

* With optional equipment
(s) Using subroutine
N Number of devices tested

	SYSTEM IDENTITY	General Automation SPC 12/10, 15, 20	General Automation SPC 16/40, 60, 80	General Automation SPC 16/45, 65, 85	General Automation 18/30	General Electric GE-PAC 3010/2
DATA STRUCTURE	Word Length, bits	8	16	16	16 + 2	32
	Operand Lengths, bits	8; 12; 16; 24	1; 8; 16	1; 8; 16	16; 32	8; 16; 32
	Inst Lengths, bits	8; 16; 24	16; 32	16; 32	16; 32	16; 32
	Floating Point Format — Fract, bits	NA	NA	NA	—	24
	Floating Point Format — Exp, bits	NA	NA	NA	—	7 + sign
CENTRAL PROCESSOR	Model Number	12/10; 12/15; 12/20	16/40; 16/60; 16/80	16/45; 16/65; 16/85	1804	3010/2
	No. of Instructions	52	86	86	32	113
	Address Bits — Memory	12	8; 16	8; 16	8; 16	8; 16
	Address Bits — Devices	3	6	6	8	8
	Indirect Addressing	Multilevel	Yes	Yes	1 level[1]	No
	No. G P Reg	4	8 + 8*	8 + 8*	1 + extension	16
	No. Index Reg	3	3 + 5*	3 + 5*	3[2]	15
	Interrupt — Lines	1	8	8	8	10
	Interrupt — Levels	1	64 std	64 std	8–976	256
	Interrupt Response Times, μsec — SIP I	45.4	24.5; 20.2; 13.6	24.5; 20.2; 13.6	14.2	0
	Interrupt Response Times, μsec — SIP II	4.3	1.98; 1.94; 1.6	2.9; 1.94; 1.6	2.4	8.0
	Fixed-Point Execute Time, μsec — c=a+b	11	10.0; 6.7; 5.6	10.0; 6.7; 5.6	10.2	9.50
	Fixed-Point Execute Time, μsec — c=ab	(s)	9.6; 17.3; 11.5	17.3; 11.5; 9.6	18.8	16.50
	Fixed-Point Execute Time, μsec — c=a/b	(s)	21.6; 14.4; 12.0	21.6; 14.4; 12.0	20.0	18.50
	Floating-Point Execute Time, μsec — c=a+b	NA	NA	NA	NA	43.25
	Floating-Point Execute Time, μsec — c=ab	NA	NA	NA	NA	74.25
	Floating-Point Execute Time, μsec — c=a/b	NA	NA	NA	NA	127.00
	Real-Time Clock	Yes	Yes	Yes	Yes	Yes
	Input/Output Channels	Programmed I/O (1 serial and 1 parallel); DMA opt [1]	Programmed I/O; DMA opt	Programmed I/O; DMA opt	Programmed I/O; up to 5 DMA	Programmed I/O; 4 DMA ports, 1 interleaved opt
WORKING STORAGE	Model Number	1211, 1215, 1220	SPC 16/40, 60, 80	SPC 16/45, 65, 85	1804	GE-PAC 3010/2
	Type of Storage	Lithium core	Core	Core	Magnetic core[3]	Core
	Number of Words — Min	4K	4K	4K	4,096	2K
	Number of Words — Max	16K[2]	16K	64K	32,768	16K
	Cycle Time, μsec	2.3	1.44; 0.96; 0.80	0.8; 0.96; 1.44	0.96	1.0
	Bits per Cycle	8	16	16	16 + 1 parity and 1 protect	8; 16
	Parity	No	Opt	Opt	Yes	Opt
	Memory Protect	Yes	Opt	Opt	Yes	Yes
ROM	Availability	No	Yes	Yes	No	Std
	Use	—	Bootstrap load	Bootstrap load	—	Instructions and interrupt
	General Features and Comments	(1) Mem Access Adapter gives DMA effect (2) 12/15 to only 8K	Core available in 4K-word modules	Core available in 4K-word modules	(1) Only for 2-word instructions (2) Only 2-word instructions can be indexed (3) 16-word MSI scratchpad memory (35-nsec cycle time)	I/O routines and interrupt service are microprogrammed to provide a variety of options

* With optional equipment
(s)Using subroutine
N Number of devices tested

		General Electric GE-PAC 4010	General Electric GE-PAC 4020	GRI Computer GRI 99, 10, 30, 40	Hewlett-Packard HP 2100A	Hewlett-Packard HP 2100S
DATA STRUCTURE	**SYSTEM IDENTITY**					
	Word Length, bits	24	24	16	16 + 1 parity	16 + 1 parity
	Operand Lengths, bits	24; 48	24; 48	16	16	16
	Inst Lengths, bits	24	24	16; 32	16; 32	16; 32
	Floating Point Format Fract, bits	17/37 + sign	7/36 + sign	23 + sign	23 + sign	23 + sign
	Exp, bits	6/9	6; 9	8	7 + sign	7 + sign
CENTRAL PROCESSOR	**Model Number**	GE-PAC 4010	GE-PAC 4020	GRI 909/10/20/30/40	2100A	2100S
	No. of Instructions	117	113	229/229/229/233	61	61 + (1)
	Address Bits Memory	14	14	16	10	10
	Devices	14	12	6	6	6
	Indirect Addressing	1 level	1 level	1 level	Multilevel	Multilevel
	No. G P Reg	1 + extension	1 + extension in core	2/2/2/8	2	2
	No. Index Reg	7 (in core)	7 (in core)	Unlimited; 2nd instrctn word	None	None
	Interrupt Lines	1	1	16	2	2
	Levels	64-128	Up to 128	No limit	60	60
	Interrupt Response Times, μsec SIP I	23.6	23.6	42.2	14.4	14.4
	SIP II	0	0	0.98	2.2	2.2
	Fixed-Point Execute Time, μsec c=a+b	9.6	9.6	15.8	5.7	5.7
	c=ab	16.9	16.9	NA	10.7	10.7
	c=a/b	20.1	20.1	NA	16.7	16.7
	Floating-Point Execute Time, μsec c=a+b	220.4	211.4	278	23-59*	23-59
	c=ab	168.4	157.4	407.8	33-41*	33-41
	c=a/b	205.4	188.4	NA	51-55*	51-55
	Real-Time Clock	Yes	Yes	Yes	Yes	Yes, std
	Input/Output Channels	Programmed I/O; 16 TIM/TOM; up to 3 DMA	Programmed I/O; 16 TIM/TOM; up to 3 DMA	Programmed I/O; DMA	Up to 45 chan; any 2 can be DMA	Up to 45 chan; any 2 can be DMA; DMA std
WORKING STORAGE	**Model Number**	GE-PAC 4010	GE-PAC 4020	GRI-909/10/20/30/40	HP 2100A	HP 2100S
	Type of Storage	Magnetic core	Magnetic core	Magnetic core	Magnetic core	Magnetic core
	Number of Words Min	16,384	8,192	1K/1K/4K/4K	4,096	16,384
	Max	32,768	32,768	4K/4K/32K/32K	32,768	32,768
	Cycle Time, μsec	1.6	1.6	1.76	0.98	0.98
	Bits per Cycle	24 + 1 parity	24 + 1 parity	16	16 + 1 parity	16 + 1 parity
	Parity	Yes	Yes	No	Yes	Yes
	Memory Protect	Yes	Yes	No	Yes	Yes
ROM	**Availability**	No	No	Yes	Up to 1,024*	1,024
	Use	—	—	Microinstructions	Microinstructions	Microinstructions[2]
	General Features and Comments	Floating-point operations are performed by quasi instructions	Floating-point operations are performed by quasi instructions	Processor is built around a universal bus to which all functional elements connect; instructions select source, destination, and operator	2100A is upward program compatible with earlier HP 2100 Series computers, uses the same peripheral devices	(1) Basic instruction set includes 2100A set and floating point hardware set (2) Software support for user-coded microprograms (assembler and loaders)

* With optional equipment
(s)Using subroutine
N Number of devices tested

		Hewlett-Packard HP 3000	Honeywell H112	Honeywell H316	Honeywell DDP-516	Honeywell 72000(1)
DATA STRUCTURE	Word Length, bits	16 + 1 parity	12	16	16	16 + 1 parity*
	Operand Lengths, bits	8; 16; 32	12	8; 16; 32[1]	8; 16; 32[1]	8; 16; 32
	Inst Lengths, bits	16	12	16	16	16
	Floating Point Format — Fract, bits	21	NA	23/39 + sign	23/39 + sign	23; 39
	Floating Point Format — Exp, bits	8 + sign	NA	8	8	8 + sign
CENTRAL PROCESSOR	Model Number	30000 A	H112	H316	DDP-516	716
	No. of Instructions	170 (all std)	37	72 + 32[2]	72 + 32[2]	78 std; 14 opt
	Address Bits — Memory	16	7	9	9	9 + sector bit
	Address Bits — Devices	—	6	6	6	6
	Indirect Addressing	Multilevel	1 level	Multilevel	Multilevel	Multilevel
	No. G P Reg	4	1	1 + extension	1 + extension	6
	No. Index Reg	2	None	1	1	2
	Interrupt — Lines	15 int; 16 ext	1	1-48	1-48	64
	Interrupt — Levels	15 int; 253 ext	1	16 + 48	16 + 48	9; 2 opt
	Interrupt Response Times, μsec — SIP I	NA	88.1	35.1	20.2	24
	Interrupt Response Times, μsec — SIP II	NA	8.1N	0.0[3]	0.0[3]	0.0
	Fixed-Point Execute Time, μsec — c=a+b	7.54 memory; 0.7 stack	17.8	14.4	8.64	6.99
	— c=ab	13.14 memory; 5.95 stack	718 (s)	20.0[1]	12.0[1]	9.36
	— c=a/b	8.75 on stack	1,003 (s)	28.8[1]	17.3[1]	12.41
	Floating-Point Execute Time, μsec — c=a+b	13.2 (avg) on stack	(1)	500.6 (s)	300.5 (s)	323.9 (s)[2]
	— c=ab	17.68 on stack	(1)	492.1 (s)[1]	295.4 (s)[1]	343.3 (s)[2]
	— c=a/b	23.63 on stack	(1)	913.6 (s)[1]	548.4 (s)[1]	1,085.4 (s)[2]
	Real-Time Clock	Opt	Opt	Opt	Opt	Opt
	Input/Output Channels	Programmed I/O; DMA	I/O bus; opt direct data channels	I/O bus; DMC* (16 subchannels); High-speed DMC* (16 subchannels)	I/O bus; DMC* (16 subchannels); DMA*	Programmed I/O; DMA; DMC*
WORKING STORAGE	Model Number	300005A (control) 300006A (core)	H112	H316	DDP-516	1201, 2022[3]
	Type of Storage	Core	Magnetic core	Magnetic core	Magnetic core	Core
	Number of Words — Min	49,152	4K	4K	4K	4K
	— Max	131,072	8K	32K	32K	64K[3]
	Cycle Time, μsec	0.980	1.69	1.6	0.96	0.775/0.855[4]/1.04[3]
	Bits per Cycle	16 + 1 parity	12	16	16	16
	Parity	Std	No	Opt	Opt	Opt
	Memory Protect	Std	No	Opt	Opt	Opt
ROM	Availability	Yes	No	No	No	Opt
	Use	CPU control	—	—	—	Loaders
	General Features and Comments	Stack processing architecture; asynch components around central data bus; core available in 8K-word modules	(1) No std floating-point subroutines provided	(1) With high-speed arithmetic option (2) Provided with options (3) With opt priority interrupt lines	(1) With high-speed arithmetic option (2) Provided with options (3) With opt priority interrupt lines	(1) Basic system for user-written executive (2) Double precision (3) For extended memory beyond 32K words (4) For 1st 32K words in extended memory systems

* With optional equipment
(s) Using subroutine
N Number of devices tested

		Honeywell System 72001,[1] 02[2]	Honeywell System 72003,[1] 05[2]	Honeywell System 72020, 21[1]	Honeywell System 72050, 73050[1]	Interdata Model 1
DATA STRUCTURE	**SYSTEM IDENTITY**					
	Word Length, bits	16 (18 with parity)	16 + 1 parity*	16 + 1 parity*	16 + 1 parity*	8
	Operand Lengths, bits	8; 16	8; 16; 32*	8; 16; 32	8; 16; 32	1; 8
	Inst Lengths, bits	16	16	16	16	8; 16
	Floating Point Format Fract, bits	23; 39	23; 39	23; 39	23; 69	—
	Exp, bits	8 + sign	8 + sign	8 + sign	8 + sign	—
CENTRAL PROCESSOR	**Model Number**	716	H316	716	716	Interdata Model 1
	No. of Instructions	78 std; 14 opt	72 + 32*	78 std; 14 opt	78 std; 14 opt	49
	Address Bits Memory	9 + sector bit	9	9 + sector bit	9 + sector bit	8
	Devices	6	6	6	6	8
	Indirect Addressing	Multilevel	Multilevel	Multilevel	Multilevel	Yes
	No. G P Reg	6	1 + extension	6	6	1
	No. Index Reg	2	1	2	2	None[1]
	Interrupt Lines	64	1-48	64	24	4-8*
	Levels	9; 2 opt	16 + 48*	9; 2 opt	9; 2 opt	4-8
	Interrupt Response Times, μsec SIP I	24	35.1	24	24	15.0
	SIP II	0	0.0[3]	0.0	0.0	0.0
	Fixed-Point Execute Time, μsec c=a+b	6.99	14.4	6.99	6.99	9.0
	c=ab	9.36	20.0*	9.36	9.36	NA
	c=a/b	12.41	28.8*	12.41	12.41	NA
	Floating-Point Execute Time, μsec c=a+b	323.9 (s)[3]	500.6 (s)	323.9 (s)[2]	323.9 (s)[2]	NA
	c=ab	343.3 (s)[3]	492.1 (s)*	343.3 (s)[2]	343.3 (s)[2]	NA
	c=a/b	1,085.4 (s)	913.6 (s)*	1,085.4 (s)[2]	1,085.4 (s)[2]	NA
	Real-Time Clock	Opt	Opt	Std	Std	Yes
	Input/Output Channels	Programmed I/O; DMA; DMC*	Programmed I/O; DMC* (16 subchannels); high-speed DMC*	Programmed I/O; DMA; DMC*	Programmed I/O; DMA; DMC*	I/O bus; up to 4 DMA (selector or universal); serial (bit) I/O port
WORKING STORAGE	**Model Number**	1201/2022[4]	700-02	1201, 2022[2]	1201, 2022[2]	Interdata Model 1
	Type of Storage	Core	Core	Core	Core	Magnetic core
	Number of Words Min	8K, 16K	12K	8K, 16K	8K 12K	2K[2]
	Max	32K/64K	32K	32K/64K[2]	64K,[2] 32K	16K
	Cycle Time, μsec	0.775 or .855[5] & 1.04[4]	1.6	0.775/0.885[3]/1.04[2]	0.775/0.855[3]/1.04[2]	1.0
	Bits per Cycle	16	16	16	16	8
	Parity	Opt	Opt	Opt	Opt	Opt
	Memory Protect	Opt	No (base sector relocation)	Opt	Opt	No
ROM	**Availability**	Opt	Opt	Opt	Opt	Yes
	Use	Loaders	Loaders	Loaders	Loaders	Program storage
	General Features and Comments	(1) CO-OP System (2) DOS-700 System (3) Double-precision numbers (4) For extended memory beyond 32K words (5) For 1st 32K words	(1) Multipurpose system (2) Batch Processing System (3) With opt priority interrupt lines	(1) Sensor-based systems (2) Extended memory for above 32K words, 72001 only (3) For 1st 32K words in extended memory systems	(1) Remote line and message concentrator systems (2) 72050 only with extended memory beyond 32K words (3) For 1st 32K words in extended memory systems	(1) Indirect addresses can be auto indexed (2) First memory module must be core, remainder can be core or ROM (3) Hardware x, ÷, or floating-point options unavailable

* With optional equipment
(s) Using subroutine
N Number of devices tested

	SYSTEM IDENTITY	Interdata Model 70	Interdata Model 74	Interdata Model 80	Interdata Model 85	IBM System/7
DATA STRUCTURE	Word Length, bits	16	16	16	16	16
	Operand Lengths, bits	8; 16	16	8; 16; 32	1; 8; 16; 32	16
	Inst Lengths, bits	16; 32	16; 32	16; 32	16; 32	16; 32
	Floating Point Format — Fract, bits	24 + sign	24 + sign	24 + sign	24 + sign	23; 31
	Floating Point Format — Exp, bits	7	8	7	7	8
CENTRAL PROCESSOR	Model Number	Interdata Model 70	Model 74	Model 80	Model 85	5010
	No. of Instructions	113	110	113	113 +[1]	39
	Address Bits — Memory	16	16	4; 16	4; 16	8; 16
	Address Bits — Devices	16	16	16	16	8
	Indirect Addressing	No	No	No	No	None
	No. G P Reg	16	16	16	16	64
	No. Index Reg	15	15	15	15	7
	Interrupt — Lines	8	1	8	8	64
	Interrupt — Levels	541	255	255	255	4
	Interrupt Response Times, μsec — SIP I	(1)	$6.25N$ [1]	(1)	(2)	0.8
	Interrupt Response Times, μsec — SIP II	(1)	9.0	(1)	(2)	0.8
	Fixed-Point Execute Time, μsec — c=a+b	9.5	9.5	3.1	3.1	2.4
	Fixed-Point Execute Time, μsec — c=ab	17.3	47.25	4.8	4.8	Subroutine
	Fixed-Point Execute Time, μsec — c=a/b	20.3	60.25	5.1	5.1	Subroutine
	Floating-Point Execute Time, μsec — c=a+b	53.5	348 (s)	17	17	NA
	Floating-Point Execute Time, μsec — c=ab	100.5	408 (s)	25.1	25.1	NA
	Floating-Point Execute Time, μsec — c=a/b	136.5	588 (s)	41	41	NA
	Real-Time Clock	Opt	Opt	Opt	Opt	None available
	Input/Output Channels	Mplxr; up to 4 DMA (selector or special purpose)	Multiplexor (2); selector opt	Programmed I/O; DMA; automatic; interleaved	Programmed I/O; DMA; automatic; interleave; selector	1; programmed I/O
WORKING STORAGE	Model Number	Model 70	M74-300 (core), M74-301 (core w/parity)	Model 80	M80-000 or 001	5010
	Type of Storage	Magnetic core	Core	MOS	MOS	Monolithic circuits
	Number of Words — Min	4,096	4,096	8,192	8K	2,048
	Number of Words — Max	32,768	32,768	32,768	32K	16,384
	Cycle Time, μsec	1.0	1.0	0.330	0.270 avg	0.400
	Bits per Cycle	16 + parity*	16	16 + 1 parity	16	16
	Parity	Opt	Opt (M74-301)	Opt	Opt	Yes, odd (2/word)
	Memory Protect	Opt	No (2)	Opt	Opt	None available
ROM	Availability	LSI bipolar	Yes	LSI bipolar	LSI bipolar; 4K bytes	None
	Use	Control memory	Control store (3)	Control memory	Dynamic Control Store (3)	—
	General Features and Comments	(1) Interrupts handled by firmware in different ways depending on coding in pointer table	(1) N = no. of registers stored and restored (2) Not planned to support RTOS (3) Includes automatic I/O firmware via interrupt system	(1) Interrupts handled by firmware in different ways; devices identified via vector table	(1) Instructions to control dynamic control store + user-defined instructions (2) Interrupts handled by firmware in different ways; devices identified by vector table	16 models available in 2K memory increments, 8 "A" and 8 "B" models; "A" models for stand-alone use, "B" models attach to IBM 1130 systems; "A" models can have communications features

* With optional equipment
(s) Using subroutine
N Number of devices tested

	SYSTEM IDENTITY		IBM 1130	IBM 1800	Lockheed Electronics MAC 16; MAC Jr	Lockheed Electronics SUE	Microdata MICRO 400
DATA STRUCTURE	Word Length, bits		16	16	16	16	8
	Operand Lengths, bits		16; 32	16; 32	16	8; 16	8
	Inst Lengths, bits		16; 32	16; 32	16	16; 32	8; 16
	Floating Point Format	Fract, bits	23; 31	23; 31	24	NA	NA
		Exp, bits	8	8	7 + sign	NA	NA
CENTRAL PROCESSOR	Model Number		1131	1801; 1802	MAC 16; MAC Jr	1110; 1111; 1112	MICRO 400
	No. of Instructions		29	33	72	68 (1110), others more	118
	Address Bits	Memory	8; 16	8; 16	9	16	8; 12
		Devices	8	8	4	16	5
	Indirect Addressing		1 level	1 level	2 levels	Multilevel	None
	No. G P Reg		2	2	1	7	7
	No. Index Reg		3	3	1	7	1 (2 opt)
	Interrupt	Lines	6	27*	4	4	1 std; 8 opt
		Levels	6	27*	4	4, unlimited sharing	Lines can be shared
	Interrupt Response Times, μsec	SIP I	2.2; 3.6	4.0[1]	6.0	NA	4.8
		SIP II	0	4.0[1]	2.0	NA	4.8
	Fixed-Point Execute Time, μsec	c=a+b	23.2; 30.2[1]	13.00[1]	6.0	10.6	6.4
		c=ab	44.5; 57.7[1]	25.75[1]	437 (s)	301.0 (s)	Subroutine
		c=a/b	98.4; 127.7[1]	55.25[1]	769 (s)	498.0 (s)	Subroutine
	Floating-Point Execute Time, μsec	c=a+b	460 (s); 597 (s)[1]	230.0[1]	NA	(s)	NA
		c=ab	560 (s); 727 (s)[1]	280.0[1]	NA	(s)	NA
		c=a/b	766 (s); 996 (s)[1]	283.0[1]	NA	(s)	NA
	Real-Time Clock		None available	None available	None available	No	Opt
	Input/Output Channels		5; model-dependent choice of devices	3 std; 6 addtnl opt; 1802 includes mag tape control	Programmed I/O; max, 2 selector data (DMA)	INFIBUS (see Comments)	Programmed std; DMA opt
WORKING STORAGE	Model Number		1131 (11 models)	1801 or 1802(1) 1803	MAC 16; MAC Jr	3311/3312	4101 (1K); 4104 (4K)
	Type of Storage		Magnetic core	Magnetic core	Magnetic core	Core	Magnetic core
	Number of Words	Min	4,096[2]	4,096 8,192	4,096[1]	4K/8K	1,024
		Max	32,768[2]	65,536 40,960	65,536	30K	65,536[1]
	Cycle Time, μsec		2.2; 3.6	2.0; 4.0 2.25	1.0	0.850; 0.950	1.6
	Bits per Cycle		16	16	16	16	8
	Parity		Yes, odd (2/word)	Yes, odd (1/word)	None	No	None
	Memory Protect		None available	Yes	None	No	None
ROM	Availability		None	None	None	Yes	Opt
	Use		—	—	—	Program security	Replacement for core
	General Features and Comments		(1) Mod 4 execution times (2) Mod 1A, 1B, 2A, 2D, 4A, 4B have 3.6-μsec cycle; Mod 1 and 4 have max 8K core; Mod 3B, 3C, 3D have 2.2-μsec cycle, min 8K core; all except Mod 1 have built-in disc drive	(1) For 2-μsec memory, double for 4-μsec memory, multiply by 1.125 for 2.25-μsec memory (2) 10 models of 1801 and 1802 P-Cs are available	(1) MAC Jr requires a memory expansion adapter to add memory to system	INFIBUS has inherent DMA facility Both ROM and RAM LSI modules available in 1K-word increments; cycle time 450-nsec per word 1111 processor for RPG; 1112 for Fortran	(1) Only 4,096 bytes can be directly addressed, rest are indexed

* With optional equipment
(s)Using subroutine
N Number of devices tested

	SYSTEM IDENTITY	Microdata MICRO 820; 821	Microdata MICRO 1620, 21	Microdata MICRO 3230 (1)	Microdata MICRO 32/S (1)	Modular Computer MODCOMP I/5, I/15
DATA STRUCTURE	Word Length, bits	8	8	16	16	16
	Operand Lengths, bits	8; 16; 24; 32	8; 16; 24; 32	Variable	1; 2; 4; 8; 16; 32	8; 16
	Inst Lengths, bits	8; 16; 24; 32; 40	16	8; 16; 24		16; 32
	Floating Point Format — Fract, bits	NA	NA	NA	NA	22/38 + sign
	Floating Point Format — Exp, bits	NA	NA	NA	NA	9
CENTRAL PROCESSOR	Model Number	820, 821	1600/10;/11;/20;/21	3200(2)	3200(2)	MODCOMP I, I/5
	No. of Instructions	102; 107(1)	107	110(3)	(3)	62; 40*
	Address Bits — Memory	15	15	16	—	16
	Address Bits — Devices	5	6	5	—	6
	Indirect Addressing	1 level	1 level	1 level	—	None
	No. G P Reg	1 + 1 ext	6	1 + ext	32	3
	No. Index Reg	1	1	1	—	3
	Interrupt — Lines	1	1	1	2	2-4*
	Interrupt — Levels	8-64	8-64	8-64	4; 1,024	128
	Interrupt Response Times, μsec — SIP I	11.4	10.30	3.1	3.1	17.6
	Interrupt Response Times, μsec — SIP II	13.20	11.88	3.6	3.6	5.1
	Fixed-Point Execute Time, μsec — $c=a+b$	15.18	13.66	4.1	4.1	7.2
	Fixed-Point Execute Time, μsec — $c=ab$	65.78	59.20	17.8	17.8	18.0*
	Fixed-Point Execute Time, μsec — $c=a/b$	93.72	84.35	25.3	25.3	24.2*
	Floating-Point Execute Time, μsec — $c=a+b$	NA	NA	NA	NA	(s)
	Floating-Point Execute Time, μsec — $c=ab$	NA	NA	NA	NA	(s)
	Floating-Point Execute Time, μsec — $c=a/b$	NA	NA	NA	NA	(s)
	Real-Time Clock	Opt	Std	Std	Opt	Opt
	Input/Output Channels	Serial TTY; DMA chan; byte I/O bus	Programmed; byte I/O; DMA chan	Programmed byte I/O; firmware block I/O DMA	Programmed I/O; firmware block I/O; DMA	Programmed I/O; 4 block transfer
WORKING STORAGE	Model Number	8208 (4K); 8288 (8K)	2204 (4K); 2208 (8K)	3230	32/S	MODCOMP I
	Type of Storage	Magnetic core	Magnetic core	MOS	MOS	Core or solid state (ss)
	Number of Words — Min	4,096	4,096	4K	4K	2K
	Number of Words — Max	32,768	32,768 (65,536 opt)	32K	128K	32K(core);16K(ss)
	Cycle Time, μsec	1.1 (0.66 access)	1.0 (0.6 access)	0.300	0.300	0.8
	Bits per Cycle	8	8	16	16	16
	Parity	No	None	No	No	Opt
	Memory Protect	None available	None available	No	Opt	None
ROM	Availability	Std	Std	4,096 words (max)	4,096 words (max)	Yes (2 types)
	Use	Control Memory	Microprogramming	Control Memory	Writable Control Store (4)	Microprogram (std), prog protect (opt)
	General Features and Comments	821 has 2 decimal arithmetic instructions	0.2-μsec ROM cycle; 2 dec. arith instructions; 768, 512, 768, and 1,024-word ROMs in respective models;"-1" series avail with extra sub-assembly slots and remote power supply; failsafe/auto-restart std	(1) Upward compatible with MICRO 800 and 1600 Series (2) Stack-oriented microprocessor with MICRO 800 and 1600 firmware added (3) Includes decimal + and -	(1) Programmed using MPL, a PL-1 derivative (2) Stack-oriented microprocessor (3) Implement MPL (4) Software supported	Designed as dedicated controller; bit and byte manipulating instructions

With optional equipment
)Using subroutine
Number of devices tested

	SYSTEM IDENTITY	Modular Computer MODCOMP II/5, 10	Modular Computer MODCOMP II/20, 25	Modular Computer MODCOMP III/5	Nuclear Data ND 812	Philips P850, 850M[1]
DATA STRUCTURE	Word Length, bits	16	16 + 1 parity*	16	12	16
	Operand Lengths, bits	8; 16; 32	8; 16; 32	8; 16; 32	12	NA
	Inst Lengths, bits	16; 32	16; 32	16; 32	12; 24	16; 32
	Floating Point Format — Fract, bits	22/38 + sign	22/38 + sign	22/38 + sign	22 + sign	NA
	Floating Point Format — Exp, bits	9	9	9	10 + sign	NA
CENTRAL PROCESSOR	Model Number	MODCOMP II, II/5	II/20, II/25	III/5, 15, 20, 30, 40, 50	88-0397	P850
	No. of Instructions	103; 34*	103; 50*	145; 26*	(129)	NA
	Address Bits — Memory	16	16	16	6; 12	NA
	Address Bits — Devices	6	6	6	4; 6	6
	Indirect Addressing	1 level	1 level	1 level	1 level	Yes
	No. G P Reg	15	15	15	2	15
	No. Index Reg	7	7	7	None (see Comments)	15
	Interrupt — Lines	3–8*	3–8*	4–32*	1	1
	Interrupt — Levels	128	128	128	1–4	1; 15*
	Interrupt Response Times, μsec — SIP I	3.2	3.2	3.2	46.0	NA
	Interrupt Response Times, μsec — SIP II	5.1	5.1	5.1	0.	NA
	Fixed-Point Execute Time, μsec — c=a+b	7.2	7.2	7.2	18.0	32.0
	Fixed-Point Execute Time, μsec — c=ab	11.0	11.0[1]	14.4	36.8	NA
	Fixed-Point Execute Time, μsec — c=a/b	24.2	14.7[1]	19.2	37.0	NA
	Floating-Point Execute Time, μsec — c=a+b	(s)	26.2*	Opt	NA	NA
	Floating-Point Execute Time, μsec — c=ab	(s)	23.9*	Opt	NA	NA
	Floating-Point Execute Time, μsec — c=a/b	(s)	24.2*	Opt	NA	NA
	Real-Time Clock	Opt	Opt	Yes*	Yes*	Yes*
	Input/Output Channels	Programmed I/O; 16 block transfer; DMA	Programmed I/O; DMP (8 chan); External DMP (4 chan)	Programmed I/O; 16 block transfer; DMA; 4 chan cont.	I/O bus; DMA controller	Programmed I/O
WORKING STORAGE	Model Number	MODCOMP II	3601, 08, 09[2]	MODCOMP III	ND 812	P850
	Type of Storage	Core or solid state (ss)	Core	Core or solid state (ss)	Core	Magnetic core
	Number of Words — Min	4K	16K	2K	4,096	512
	Number of Words — Max	32K(core);16K (ss)	65K	65K(core); 16K (ss)	16,384	2,048
	Cycle Time, μsec	0.8	0.800	0.8	2.0	1.6
	Bits per Cycle	16	16	16	12	8
	Parity	Opt	Opt	Yes	None	No
	Memory Protect	Opt	Opt[2]	Yes*	None	No
ROM	Availability	Yes (2 types)	Yes	Yes (2 types)	None	None
	Use	Microprogram (std), prog protect (opt)	Control Memory	Microprogram (std), prog protect (opt)	—	—
	General Features and Comments	Bit and byte manipulating instructions; 0.2-μsec ROM cycle time	(1) Multiply/divide std on II/25 and opt on II/20 (2) 4-port memory option and system protect available for II/20 only	MODCOMP III/70 provides multiprocessor configuration (2 CPUs); bit and byte manipulating instructions; 0.2-μsec ROM cycle time; floating-point hardware opt	2 words in each memory page (4,096 words) usable as auto-index locations when indirectly addressed	All accesses to memory are for one 8-bit byte (1) OEM version

* With optional equipment
(s) Using subroutine
N Number of devices tested

	SYSTEM IDENTITY	Philips P880	PRIME Computer 100	PRIME Computer 200	Raytheon Computer 704	Raytheon Computer 707 (1)
DATA STRUCTURE	Word Length, bits	16 + 2	16	16 + 1 parity	16 + 2*	16 + 2 parity
	Operand Lengths, bits	NA	8; 16; 32	8; 16; 32	8; 16	8; 16
	Inst Lengths, bits	16; 32	16	16	16	16
	Floating Point Format — Fract, bits	NA	7; 23; 39 + sign	7; 23; 39 + sign	23; 30; 45	23; 30; 46
	Floating Point Format — Exp, bits	NA	8	8	8 + sign	8 + sign
CENTRAL PROCESSOR	Model Number	P880	111, 112, 115, 116	211-218, 221-224	704	707/01;707/01 MP[2]
	No. of Instructions	53; 59*	118	118	74; 76*	76 + 7 opt (3)
	Address Bits — Memory	8; 16	9	9	11	11
	Address Bits — Devices	NA	6	6	8	8
	Indirect Addressing	NA	Yes	Yes	None	No
	No. G P Reg	NA	6	6	1	1
	No. Index Reg	3	4	4	1	1
	Interrupt — Lines	16-40*	1	1	1-16*	1
	Interrupt — Levels	NA	4000	64	1-16*	8-16
	Interrupt Response Times, μsec — SIP I	NA	NA	NA	10.0	7.2
	Interrupt Response Times, μsec — SIP II	NA	NA	NA	4.0N	2.7
	Fixed-Point Execute Time, μsec — c=a+b	4.48		6.55	12.0	10.8
	Fixed-Point Execute Time, μsec — c=ab	12.2		15.07	98.0 (s); 24.0*	18.0
	Fixed-Point Execute Time, μsec — c=a/b	12.7		19.31	185 (s); 24.0*	18.0
	Floating-Point Execute Time, μsec — c=a+b	24.3*	Subroutine	Subroutine	136 (s)	165 (s) (4)
	Floating-Point Execute Time, μsec — c=ab	32.6*	Subroutine	Subroutine	386 (s); 219 (s)*	218 (s) (4)
	Floating-Point Execute Time, μsec — c=a/b	34.5*	Subroutine	Subroutine	600 (s); 263 (s)*	248 (s) (4)
	Real-Time Clock	Yes*	Opt	Opt	Yes*	Opt
	Input/Output Channels	I/O bus; 8- or 16-bit multiplex channel*; simplex channel*	Programmed I/O bus; DMA	Programmed I/O bus; DMA	I/O bus; DMA channel*	Programmed I/O; DMA (8 levels)*
WORKING STORAGE	Model Number	P880	170, 171	270, 271	71401	71701
	Type of Storage	Core	MOS	MOS	Core	Core[2]
	Number of Words — Min	8,192	4,096	4,096	4,096	8,192
	Number of Words — Max	65,536	32,768	65,536[1]	32,768	32,768
	Cycle Time, μsec	0.64	1.0	0.75	1.0	0.900
	Bits per Cycle	16	16	16	16	16 + 2 parity
	Parity	Yes	No	Yes	Yes*	Std
	Memory Protect	Yes*	No	No	None	Std
ROM	Availability	None	No	No	None	None
	Use	—	—	—	—	—
	General Features and Comments	Bit addressing		(1) Processor models 221-224 only	Opt DMA channel can handle up to 6 controllers at 665,000 words/sec	(1) Upward I/O & software compatible with 700 Series; ruggedized system (2) Up to 4 memory ports/module; requires 707/01 MP (3) Includes sq root & trig functions (4) 31-bit fraction

With optional equipment
Using subroutine
Number of devices tested

116 *Auerbach on Minicomputers*

SYSTEM IDENTITY	Spiras Systems SPIRAS-65	Systems Engineering Labs SEL 71/72(1)	Texas Instruments TI 960A	Texas Instruments 980A	UniComp Comp-16
DATA STRUCTURE					
Word Length, bits	16	16	16 + 1 parity	16 + 1 parity	16
Operand Lengths, bits	16; 32; 64	8; 16	1–16	1; 8; 16; 32	16
Inst Lengths, bits	16; 32	16	32	16; 32; 48	16
Floating Point Format — Fract, bits	45/22 + sign	30 + sign	24	24; 32	24
Floating Point Format — Exp, bits	15/7 + sign	15 + sign	8	8	7
CENTRAL PROCESSOR					
Model Number	SPIRAS-65	SEL 71/72	960A	980A	16-001
No. of Instructions	125	163	78; 14*	98	31
Address Bits — Memory	10; 16	7	16	8; 16	8
Address Bits — Devices	6	7	10	8	8
Indirect Addressing	Multilevel	1 level	1 level	1 level	1 level
No. G P Reg	1	1 + extension(2)	16 (2 sets of 8)	8	1; 4*
No. Index Reg	1	1 (preindexing); 1 (postindexing) (2)	16 (2 sets of 8)	1 + base	6 in memory
Interrupt — Lines	1; modules of 8*	1	1 int; 2 ext	1 int; 2 ext	1-64*
Interrupt — Levels	1; modules of 8*	384	1/line	4-64	1
Interrupt Response Times, μsec — SIP I	8.0	21.0	36.9	NA	87.7
Interrupt Response Times, μsec — SIP II	16.2	5.3	4.4N	NA	5.0 + 6.0N
Fixed-Point Execute Time, μsec — c=a+b	16.2	15.0	12.7	7.75	9.3
Fixed-Point Execute Time, μsec — c=ab	30.6	21.0*	19.4	12.00	330 (s); 30.3*
Fixed-Point Execute Time, μsec — c=a/b	33.8	21.5*	21.3	12.25	450 (s); 30.7*
Floating-Point Execute Time, μsec — c=a+b	57.6	417	NA	(s)	NA
Floating-Point Execute Time, μsec — c=ab	138.6	657*	NA	(s)	NA
Floating-Point Execute Time, μsec — c=a/b	138.6	757*	NA	(s)	NA
Real-Time Clock	Yes*	Yes	Opt	No	Yes*
Input/Output Channels	I/O bus; DMA chan*	Programmed I/O; DMA	Programmed I/O (4 ports std, 252 opt); DMA (std, 5 opt)	Programmed I/O (4-256 ports); DMA (1-8 ports)	I/O bus; DMA chan*
WORKING STORAGE					
Model Number	SPIRAS-65	SEL 71/72	226844 (MOS); 246692 (core)	980A	Comp-16
Type of Storage	Core	Core/SC	MOS std; core opt	Semiconductor	Core
Number of Words — Min	4,096	4,096	4,096	4,096	4,096
Number of Words — Max	65,536	65,536	65,568	65,536	65,536
Cycle Time, μsec	1.8	0.88	0.75 (MOS);0.96(core)	0.750	0.89
Bits per Cycle	16	16	16 + 1 parity	16	16
Parity	None	Opt	Std	Std	Yes*
Memory Protect	Yes	Std	Std	Std	Yes*
ROM					
Availability	512 words	No	None	Std	Std
Use	Microprogramming	—	—	Bootstrap loader	Bootstrap loader
General Features and Comments	ROM uses 32-bit words; ROM bootstrap loader std	(1) 71 does not have virtual memory addressing; 72 with virtual memory (2) Located in core; optionally available as IC flip-flop	Times given are for 960A with MOS memory	Opt battery pack provides standby power to protect 16K words of memory for 2 weeks; 32K words of memory fit in mainframe chassis	Opt floating-point hardware

* With optional equipment
(s)Using subroutine
N Number of devices tested

	SYSTEM IDENTITY	UniComp Comp-18	Univac 6135	Univac 6140/6145[1]	Varian Data Varian V73	Varian Data 520/i
DATA STRUCTURE	Word Length, bits	18	16 + 1 parity + 1 protect	16 + 1 parity	16	8 + 1*
	Operand Lengths, bits	18	16; 32	8; 16; 32	16	8; 16; 24; 32
	Inst Lengths, bits	18	16/32	16/32	16; 32	8; 16; 24
	Floating Point Format — Fract, bits	28	23/53 + 1 sign	23/53 + 1 sign	22	24
	Floating Point Format — Exp, bits	7	8	8	8	7
CENTRAL PROCESSOR	Model Number	18-001	6135	6140/6145	7000; 7001	520/i
	No. of Instructions	31	56	71/75	159 std; no limit*	60
	Address Bits — Memory	10	8; 15	8; 15	15; 18*	10
	Address Bits — Devices	10	6	7	6	5
	Indirect Addressing	1 level	Multilevel	Multilevel	Multilevel	Multilevel
	No. G P Reg	1; 4*	1 + extension	1 + extension	3	8
	No. Index Reg	6 in memory	3	3	2	2
	Interrupt — Lines	1-64*	3	1	1 std; 64 opt	2 int*; 11 ext
	Interrupt — Levels	1	5 std; 126 opt	40/64	1 std; 64 opt	2 int*; 4 ext
	Interrupt Response Times, μsec — SIP I	87.7	21.8	NA	NA	21.0
	Interrupt Response Times, μsec — SIP II	5.0 + 6.0N	0	NA	NA	3.0 + 7.5N
	Fixed-Point Execute Time, μsec — c=a+b	9.3	8.8	9.0/5.69	5.94	19.5
	Fixed-Point Execute Time, μsec — c=ab	360 (s); 31.1*	12.8 avg	12.85/9.47	12.5	190 (s)
	Fixed-Point Execute Time, μsec — c=a/b	505 (s); 31.6*	16.1 avg	16.05/14.53	12.5	400 (s)
	Floating-Point Execute Time, μsec — c=a+b	NA	78.0 avg	(S)/18.27	NA	740 (s)
	Floating-Point Execute Time, μsec — c=ab	NA	178 avg	(S)/24.37	NA	1,420 (s)
	Floating-Point Execute Time, μsec — c=a/b	NA	142 avg	(S)/37.97	NA	1,760 (s)
	Real-Time Clock	Yes*	Yes	Yes	Yes*	Yes*
	Input/Output Channels	I/O bus; DMA chan*	XIO; MUX; Word/Byte(1)	PIO; up to 7/18 DMA	Programmed I/O; DMA; high-speed DMA; PMA	I/O bus; DMA chan
WORKING STORAGE	Model Number	Comp-18	MM-03	6140/6145	7030, 2, 4, 7 (MOS); 7020, 4 (core)	520/i
	Type of Storage	Core	Core memory	Core	Core; MOS; both	Core
	Number of Words — Min	4,096	8,192	16K/32K	4K (core), 1K (MOS)	4,096
	Number of Words — Max	262,144	32,768	31K/131K(2)	262K	32,768
	Cycle Time, μsec	0.89	0.65	1.0; 0.650	0.660 (core); 0.330 (MOS)	1.5
	Bits per Cycle	18	18	16	16	8
	Parity	None	Yes	Yes	Opt (2 bits/word)	Yes*
	Memory Protect	Yes*	Yes	Yes	Opt	None
ROM	Availability	Std	No	None	Yes	None
	Use	Bootstrap loader	—	—	Writable control storage	—
	General Features and Comments	Fast Fourier transform analyzer configures with Comp-18 processor; special I/O opt multiply/divide hardware, transform processor; complex converter and multiplier	(1) MUX has 16 sub-channels; 1 a priority subchannel; only 1 MUX per memory bus; up to 6 W/B chan per memory bus	(1) Upward compatible with 6135 (2) 169K with dual-processor configurations	Microprogrammed processor; 1st 512-word module emulates 620 processors; 2 addtnl modules opt; 16 GP registers avlble to microprogram; memory has 2 entry ports	8- or 16-bit I/O transfers; dual mode operation (4 registers in each environment)

* With optional equipment
s) Using subroutine
N Number of devices tested

	SYSTEM IDENTITY		Varian Data 620/f-100	Varian Data 620/L-100	Varisystems PAC-16	Wang Labs WANG 3300	Westinghouse 2500
DATA STRUCTURE	Word Length, bits		16	16	16	16	16
	Operand Lengths, bits		16	16	8	8; 16	16; 32
	Inst Lengths, bits		16; 32	16; 32	16	16	16
	Floating Point Format	Fract, bits	22	22	NA	32	24
		Exp, bits	8	8	NA	8	7
CENTRAL PROCESSOR	Model Number		620/f	620/L	PAC-16	WANG 3300 BASIC	25 CPU
	No. of Instructions		142 + 8*	107 + 18*	35; 38	72	44
	Address Bits	Memory	9; 15*	9; 15*	12	8	8
		Devices	6	6	8	4	7; 15
	Indirect Addressing		4 levels	Multilevel	None	1 level	1 level
	No. G P Reg		2	2	1	2	1
	No. Index Reg		2	2	NA	None	2
	Interrupt	Lines	1–68*	1–64*	2*	8	2 int; 1 ext
		Levels	1–68*	1–64*	NA	8	2 int; 1 ext
	Interrupt Response Times, μsec	SIP I	33.0	61.2	NA	24	17.7
		SIP II	0.0	0.0	NA	10	7.3
	Fixed-Point Execute Time, μsec	c=a+b	6.75	16.2	9.	18	7.2
		c=ab	308 (s); 14.25*	739 (s); 34.2*	(s)	NA	35.5
		c=a/b	157 (s); 14.25*	378 (s); 39.6*	(s)	NA	46.9
	Floating-Point Execute Time, μsec	c=a+b	177 (s)	425 (s)	NA	1,000 (s)	23*
		c=ab	187 (s)	448 (s)	NA	4,000 (s)	32*
		c=a/b	260 (s)	623 (s)	NA	4,000 (s)	32*
	Real-Time Clock		Yes*	Yes*	Yes	No	Yes*
	Input/Output Channels		I/O bus; DMA channel; buffer interlace controller*	I/O bus; DMA channel; buffer interlace controller*	I/O bus; DMA chan*	I/O bus; DMA chan	I/O bus; DMA chan
WORKING STORAGE	Model Number		620/f	620/L	PAC-16	WANG 3300	25MEM
	Type of Storage		Core	Core	Core	Core	Core
	Number of Words	Min	4,096	4,096	512	4,096	4,096
		Max	32,768	32,768	NA	65,536	65,536
	Cycle Time, μsec		0.75	1.8	1.0	1.6	0.75
	Bits per Cycle		16	16	8	8	16
	Parity		None	None	NA	No	Yes*
	Memory Protect		Yes*	Yes*	NA	Yes*	Yes*
ROM	Availability		Opt	None	NA	None	Opt
	Use		Programming	—	NA	—	Bootstrap loader
	General Features and Comments		Upward compatible with 620/i; priority memory access option shares memory lines with up to 4 devices	Lower-cost version of 620/i; completely compatible with 620/i; opt extended addressing for direct addressing of entire memory	Byte-oriented processor	Time sharing system with up to 16 ASR 3301 Selectric user terminals	Privileged control and I/O instructions; 10 fast access memory locations (registers) with 0.45-μsec access time; opt floating-point hardware

* With optional equipment
(s) Using subroutine
N Number of devices tested

DATA STRUCTURE	**SYSTEM IDENTITY**		Xerox Sigma 3
	Word Length, bits		16 + 1
	Operand Lengths, bits		16; 32*
	Inst Lengths, bits		16
	Floating Point Format	**Fract, bits**	24
		Exp, bits	8
CENTRAL PROCESSOR	**Model Number**		Sigma 3
	No. of Instructions		36; 43*
	Address Bits	**Memory**	8
		Devices	8
	Indirect Addressing		1 level
	No. G P Reg		3
	No. Index Reg		2
	Interrupt	**Lines**	4–20* int; 0–96* ext
		Levels	4–116*
	Interrupt Response Times, μsec	**SIP I**	NA
		SIP II	NA
	Fixed-Point Execute Time, μsec	**c=a+b**	5.85
		c=ab	203 (s); 11.7*
		c=a/b	272 (s); 12.0*
	Floating-Point Execute Time, μsec	**c=a+b**	125 (s)
		c=ab	713 (s); 178 (s)*
		c=a/b	713 (s); 157 (s)*
	Real-Time Clock		Yes*
	Input/Output Channels		Byte I/O chan; direct I/O chan
WORKING STORAGE	**Model Number**		Sigma 3
	Type of Storage		Core
	Number of Words	**Min**	8,192
		Max	65,536
	Cycle Time, μsec		0.975
	Bits per Cycle		16
	Parity		Yes*
	Memory Protect		Yes*
ROM	**Availability**		None
	Use		—
	General Features and Comments		Entirely upward compatible with Sigma 2; max 28 I/O chan, each controlled by 2 registers

With optional equipment
)Using subroutine
Number of devices tested

APPENDIX B: ALGOL

The ALGOL language, originally called IAL (International Algebraic Language) is the only computer language developed by an international committee. The original IAL became known as ALGOL 58; it was revised in 1960 and renamed ALGOL 60. Most minicomputer ALGOL compilers are based on the ALGOL 60 language. A later revision changed ALGOL 60 to ALGOL 68. To date, ISO (International Standards Organization) has not adopted a Standard ALGOL, although one has been proposed.

Because the original stated purpose of the language was to describe computational processes that were machine-independent, the language included no input/output (I/O) statements, which are generally machine-dependent. Thus, each compiler implements a unique set of I/O statements. The proposed ISO Standard ALGOL provides two types of I/O procedures, which will be discussed later.

Although it was not implemented on many computers until recent years, ALGOL has contributed heavily to language development, both directly and indirectly:

1. The development of NELLIAC, MAD, CLIP, and JOVIAL was stimulated indirectly by ALGOL 58.

2. It defined language syntax formally.

3. Block structure that defines scope of variables was introduced by ALGOL.

4. It introduced recursive procedures.

5. It showed how a language could express complex processes or computations simply.

6. The development of new techniques to implement languages was a direct contribution.

The ALGOL language has been far more important than is indicated by the number of compilers produced in the United States. Designers of other languages have borrowed from ALGOL and many extensions to it have been implemented: Formula ALGOL, LISP, AED, SFD-ALGOL, SIMULA, DIAMAG, GPL, and Extended ALGOL.

John W. Backus* described ALGOL 58 (IAL) in 1959 in what has become known as BNF (Backus Normal Form or Backus-Naur Form). His work stimulated interest in using meta-languages to formalize the description of programs.

The block structure of ALGOL in which each block is defined by a BEGIN and an END statement delimits the scope of a variable. Blocks can be nested within blocks without limitation on the number of nested levels.

Recursive procedures were first introduced by ALGOL and are extensively used in multiprogramming environments today.

Although ALGOL is a good language for expressing algorithms simply, the compiler implementation is not easy. Nesting, recursion, dynamic storage allocation, and other features that were difficult to implement stimulated the use of pushdown stacks, multiple index registers, and other programming techniques that effected changes in hardware design.

Because ALGOL is used extensively abroad, United States computer manufacturers can export their systems more effectively if the software includes an ALGOL compiler. Thus, the number of systems with ALGOL compilers is increasing rapidly.

FEATURES OF ALGOL

The character set for ALGOL is listed in Table B-1. As a practical matter, the lower-case characters are not contained in many compilers because the popular Teletype terminals used for most computers do not have lower-case characters. The operators listed in Table B-2 and the ALGOL words listed in Table B-3 are also part of the character set. The ALGOL words, including apostrophes, are treated as a single character in the language. These words may also be used as labels by the program, but in this case the apostrophes are dropped.

Who's Who in Computers and Data Processing 1971, Volume 3, *New York Times* Book and Educational Division, New York and *Computers and Automation*, Berkeley Enterprises Inc., New York.

Table B-1. ALGOL Character Set

SYMBOL		USE
Letters A through Z (both upper and lower cases)		To form identifiers and strings
Digits 0 through 9		To form numbers, identifiers, and strings
Logical values 'TRUE', 'FALSE'		Constants
Punctuation		
.	period	Decimal point in numbers
,	comma	Separator for items in a list
:	colon	Separator for statement label
;	semicolon	Separator for statements
(	left parenthesis	Enclose parameter lists; indicate
)	right parenthesis	expression evaluation
[	left bracket	Enclose subscripts
]	right bracket	
"	left string quote	Enclose strings
\	right string quote	
'	apostrophe	Enclose words with fixed meaning
← or :=	arrow or colon, equal	Assignment operator
	blank space	Space within strings

ALGOL Programs

The six statement types for ALGOL are listed in Table B-4. Programs can be coded on 72-column coding forms in free form. Blanks are ignored by the compiler, so blanks can be inserted anywhere they are needed to make the code readable. A single statement or declaration can use as many lines as needed, or any number of statements or declarations can be written on one line. Labels (identifiers) can be any length and consist of any characters in the set, but must start with an alphabetic character. Table B-5 lists the identifiers that are recommended as reserved.

Because of the block structure of ALGOL, with each block enclosed in 'BEGIN' and 'END' statements, it is useful to indent them according to their level in the overall program.

The semicolon (;) separates statements, and the colon (:) separates a statement label from a statement. A comment can be inserted in a statement between 'COMMENT' and the semicolon (;).

Each program block consists of 'BEGIN', declarations, statements, and 'END'; the declarations must precede the statements. Declarations set the stage for the processing done by the statements in the blocks.

Table B-2. ALGOL Operators

SYMBOL	DEFINITION
Arithmetic	
+	Add
−	Subtract
*	Multiply
/	Divide
÷	Divide (integer)
↑	Exponential
Relational	
'LS'	Less than ($<$)
'LQ'	Less than or equal to ($\leq$)
'EQ'	Equal to ($=$)
'GQ'	Greater than or equal to ($\geq$)
'GR'	Greater than ($>$)
'NQ'	Not equal to ($\neq$)
Logical	
'EQV'	Equivalent ($\equiv$)
'IMP'	Implies ($\supset$)
'OR'	Or ($\wedge$)
'AND'	And ($\vee$)
'NOT'	Negation ($\neg$)

Table B-3. ALGOL Words with Fixed Meaning

'ARRAY'	'LABEL'
'BEGIN'	'OWN'
'BOOLEAN'	'PROCEDURE
'COMMENT'	'REAL'
'DO'	'STEP
'ELSE'	'STRING'
'END'	'SWITCH'
'FOR'	'THEN'
'GOTO'	'UNTIL'
'IF'	'VALUE'
'INTEGER'	'WHILE'

Table B-4. ALGOL Statement Types

NAME	USE
Procedure	Defines a sequence of statements that can be called by name.
Assignment	Assigns a value to a variable or a group of variables; the value can be calculated using the operators and other variables.
Conditional	Controls the execution of individual or groups of statements in accordance with specified conditions.
'GOTO'	Transfers control.
Dummy	Performs no operation except that it labels a place in the program.
'FOR'	Iterates a sequence of statements.

Table B-5. Recommended ALGOL Reserved Identifiers*

IDENTIFIER	MEANING
ABS	Absolute value
ARCTAN	Arctangent
COS	Cosine
ENTIER	The integral part
EXP	Exponential function
LN	Natural logarithm
SIGN	Sign
SIN	Sine
SQRT	Square root

*Other identifiers will be reserved for I/O for a particular compiler.

Declarations

There are four kinds of declarations:

1. 'ARRAY' defines an array, dimensions, and data type.
2. 'PROCEDURE' defines a subroutine that can be called by name.
3. 'SWITCH' specifies control parameters for program sequencing.
4. Type specifies data type for variables: 'BOOLEAN', 'INTEGER', 'REAL'.

The 'ARRAY' declarations are of the form

Type 'ARRAY' b (or $B[c]$).

Type can be 'BOOLEAN', 'INTEGER' or 'REAL'. If no type is specified, the default type is 'REAL'. The array specifications can be of the form b or $B[c]$ where b or c is the array description and B is the array name.

The array description is of the form $d:e$, where d and e represent the lower and upper subscript bounds; they can be arithmetic expressions. Arrays can have n dimensions, which are separated by commas. Thus, an array can have a descriptor $d_1 : e_1, d_2 : e_2, \ldots d_n : e_n$. The lower-bound value cannot exceed the upper bound value.

'PROCEDURE' declarations can be in one of the following forms:

1. 'PROCEDURE' name; s
2. 'PROCEDURE' name (parameters); s
3. 'PROCEDURE' name (parameters) specification list; s
4. 'PROCEDURE' name (parameters) 'VALUE' list; specification list; s

The name is the procedure identifier and s represents the statements in the procedure. If the procedure has parameters, they are enclosed in parentheses and separated by a comma or by ")B:(", where B is any sequence of letters that have no functional value but are for description or comments. Parameters can be a variable, an array switch or procedure identifier, or a label. The statement s can be a simple or compound statement or a block. In any case, it acts like a block and limits the scope of its identifiers.

The statements in s can use any identifier if it is declared in the procedure. If the procedure or in the block that called the procedure.

The specification list describes the form of the parameters: 'REAL', 'INTEGER' or 'BOOLEAN'. The 'VALUE' list assigns actual parameters to the formal parameters.

If the procedure is a function and the procedure identifier represents a value in the statement that called it, the 'PROCEDURE' is preceded by the data type, 'INTEGER', 'REAL', or 'BOOLEAN'.

The 'SWITCH' declaration is used to define alternate paths for the 'GOTO' statement. It has the following form.

'SWITCH' name $p_1, p_2 \ldots, p_n$.

The name is the switch identifier that is replaced by paths $p_1, p_2 \ldots, p_n$ in the calling statement. The path p_i can be a statement label, a switch identifier, or a conditional Boolean expression that produces two alternate paths. Each path is associated with a positive integer (p_1 with 1, p_2 with 2, up to p_n with n, and the 'GOTO' statement using the switch specifies which path is selected.

The type declaration specifies the data type of variables. It has the form

Type $v_1, v_2, \ldots v_n$

The type is 'REAL', 'INTEGER' or 'BOOLEAN', and $v_1, v_2, \ldots v_n$ are the variable identifiers. All variables must be declared, and no variable can appear in more than one type declaration within a block. The declaration holds only for the block containing the declaration. It is valid, however, for sublevel blocks unless redeclared in the sublevel block. When exiting from a block, all variables declared in that block are undefined or revert to the type declaration of a higher-level block.

The 'OWN' type allows retaining previous values of variables when re-entering a block. The variables are still undefined outside the block. The form of 'OWN' requires the specification of the variable type, 'INTEGER', 'REAL' or 'BOOLEAN':

'OWN' Type $v_1, v_2, \ldots v_n$;

Statements

The assignment statement is used to perform numerical calculations or Boolean operations and to assign values to variables. A procedure identifier can be used to assign a value if it is a procedure that evaluates a function.

The simple assignment statement has the form

a ← b ← c ← d ← e;

or

a: = b: = c: = d: = e;

All variables a, b, c, and d are assigned the value of e, which can be a literal, an arithmetic, or Boolean expression, or a procedure identifier. All variables and the expression e must be of the same type: 'REAL', 'INTEGER', or 'BOOLEAN'. Expressions are evaluated from left to right.

To provide a choice of values assigned to a variable, the assignment statement can include 'IF', 'THEN', 'ELSE' clauses:

a ← b ← c ← d ← 'IF' f 'THEN' e 'ELSE' g;

This means that the Boolean expression f is evaluated; if it is 'TRUE', the expression e is evaluated and the value assigned to a, b, c, and d. If f is 'FALSE', the expression g is evaluated and the value assigned to a, b, c, and d.

More than one 'IF' clause can be included in the assignment statement:

a ← b ← c ← d ← 'IF' f 'THEN' e 'ELSE' 'IF' h 'THEN' g 'ELSE' i;

A dummy statement is used to place a label in a program.

(label) : ;

The label has the same form as any other label.

In its simplest form, the 'FOR' statement provides a way to execute a statement with a specified value of the controlled variable. It has the following form.

'FOR' v ← e 'DO' s;

The v is called the controlled variable, e is an expression, and s can be a simple or compound statement or a block of statements. The statement s is executed with the value of e assigned to v.

To iterate the statement s a specified number of times, the 'FOR' statement has the following form:

'FOR' v ← e_1 'STEP' e_2 'UNTIL' e_3 'DO' s;

In this case, e_1 is the initial value of v, e_2 is the increment added to v for each iteration, and e_3 is the final value of v. If s is to be executed 10 times, e_1 and e_2 are 1 and e_3 is 10. Because the format of 'FOR' is general, e_2 can be positive or negative, so v can be incremented or decremented for each iteration of s.

A 'WHILE' clause can control the iteration of s in a 'FOR' statement:

'FOR' v ← e 'WHILE' b 'DO' s;

In this case the expression e is evaluated and its value assigned to v. The Boolean expression b is evalued; if it is 'TRUE', statement s is executed; if it is 'FALSE', the statement following statement s is executed.

The normal sequence is to execute one statement after another. The 'GOTO' statement provides an unconditional transfer of control in the following form:

'GOTO' a;

The a represents a statement label; thus control transfers to the statement labeled a.

The 'GOTO' statement can transfer control to a switch:

'GOTO' sw (p);

In this case, p is an expression, which is evaluated, and sw is a switch designator or name. The value of p must be an integer, and it cannot fall outside the range of sw. In other words, if sw is a three-way switch, the value of p must be 1, 2, or 3.

The 'GOTO' statement can transfer control conditionally:

'GOTO' 'IF' a 'THEN' b 'ELSE' c;

The Boolean expression *a* is evaluated. If it is 'TRUE', control is transferred to the statement labeled *b*; if it is 'FALSE', to the statement labeled *c*.

Input-Output

Because ALGOL 60 had no input-output provisions, each ALGOL compiler had its own way of handling I/O, and usually procedures were added to the language. These procedures could be 'READ', 'WRITE', 'FORMAT', and so forth. Two levels of input-output procedures have been proposed for ALGOL 68; one level is a subset of the other. The subset has been called the "Primitive" procedures. The full set is similar to input-output facilities in COBOL.

The following primitive procedures are proposed:

- 'INSYMBOL'
- 'OUTSYMBOL'   Provides communication between a peripheral device and the variables in a program.

- 'LENGTH'   Defines length of a string.

- 'INREAL'
- 'OUTREAL'   Transfers real data between the peripheral and memory.

- 'INARRAY'
- 'OUTARRAY'   Transfers an array between a peripheral and memory.

The ALGOL* compiler implemented by the Data General Corporation for the Nova/Supernova computers provides five input-output procedures.

1. 'OPEN' (a,b): Opens a file where *a* designates one of eight channels that can be associated with a file and *b* gives the file name.
2. 'CLOSE' (a): Closes a file; *a* designates the channel associated with the file.
3. 'READ' (a,b): Reads a file; *a* designates the channel associated with the file and *b* is the input data list.
4. 'WRITE' (a, b): Writes a file; *a* designates the channel associated with the file and *b* is the output data list of variables and constants.
5. 'OUTPUT' (a,b,c): Outputs a formatted file; *a* designates channel associated with the file, *b* specifies the format, and *c* is the variable list.

---

*Nova ALGOL Reference Manual 093-000052-00, Data General Corporation, Southboro, Mass., 1970.

APPENDIX C: BASIC

The Beginner's All-Purpose Symbolic Instruction Code (BASIC) was developed at Dartmouth College in Hanover, New Hampshire, under the direction of Professors John G. Kemeny and Thomas E. Kurtz. The language compiler and related executive routines were implemented in 1965 for the GE-235 and DATANET-30.* The BASIC system was conceived as an easy-to-learn compiler language geared for scientific applications. As such, the instruction set is not large. It has gained fairly wide acceptance for commercial applications; most time-sharing bureaus report that BASIC use already exceeds FORTRAN and the gap is widening.

The syntax and functional capabilities of BASIC are explained here. The version described is similar to the original implementation, but it has been delineated by the Auerbach editorial staff, since there has been no official standardization to date. Most time-sharing services offer BASIC as it is detailed in this discussion, but major extensions to the language have been implemented by some companies. These will be discussed in the concluding section of this Appendix.

This description is an explanation of BASIC; it is not intended to define the BASIC language nor to provide a tutorial introduction to it for time-sharing systems.

---

*Trademark of General Electric.

FEATURES OF BASIC

Some of the terms that will be referred to in subsequent discussion are defined as follows:

- A *program* is a set of directions written in the BASIC language that indicates to the computer what processes to follow to solve a given problem.

- A *statement* is a direction given in a program. In consists, in BASIC, of a line number plus a line of type.

- *Variables* are named quantities that are given or assigned values during program execution.

- *Expressions* designate the series of operations, such as arithmetic evaluation, to be performed. They contain numeric quantities, variables, and/or arithmetic operators.

- *Loop processing* is the means of repeating similar program operations without reentering program statements.

- The BASIC *compiler* is the part of the computer system that translates commands into language intelligible to the computer.

Standard features of the BASIC language may be divided functionally into those relating to program form, those indicating data types, expressions, statements, and procedures and subprograms.

A statement in BASIC consists of (1) a statement label, (2) a special BASIC word, (3) symbolic names, and (4) optionally, one or more operators. These quantities are generally composed of alphabetic characters, the digits 0 through 9, and commonly accepted special characters, some of which are listed in Table C-1. Statements in BASIC are placed one per line. This line is up to 72 characters long and is generally terminated on time-sharing systems by an end-of-line flag such as a carriage return. Blanks or spaces are significant to the line count, but are ignored in the syntax of the language; that is, the statements are in free format.

Statement labels begin each line and consist of one to five numerical characters. Symbolic names are characters that represent data or variables whose arithmetic value is modified or assigned during the processing of a BASIC program. These names take the form of an alphabetic character or an alphabetic character followed by a numerical digit. If the symbol's name refers to an array (an ordered set of data), the form of the name is restricted to a single letter.

The BASIC language allows a single data type: real. Real numbers are

Table C-1. Special Characters in BASIC

CHARACTER	NAME OF CHARACTER
	Blank
+	Plus
—	Minus
=	Equals
/	Slash
*	Asterisk
(	Left parenthesis
)	Right parenthesis
.	Decimal point
,	Comma
$	Dollar sign

computer approximations of the values of arithmetically real or integral quantities. Decimal points may be omitted for integral values. The precision of the numbers stored internally in the computer is dependent upon the type of processor. In BASIC, the number of output digits printed is preset, but the programmer may change it on some systems.

Expressions are parts of statements that specify operational action between variables, and may specify arithmetic or relational action. Table C-2 lists the allowable BASIC operators, which form expressions when combined with legal BASIC symbolic names.

The BASIC language contains two types of statements: executable and nonexecutable. Executable statements specify actions, whereas nonexecutable statements specify the arrangement or values of data. Certain

Table C-2. BASIC Operators

TYPE	OPERATOR	FUNCTION
Arithmetic	+	Addition, positive element
	—	Subtraction, negative element
	*	Multiplication
	/	Division
	↑	Exponentiation
Relational	<	Less than
	>	Greater than
	<=	Less than or equal to
	>=	Greater than or equal to
	=	Equals
	<>	Not equal to

English language words are used in BASIC to indicate actions to be performed during processing of executable statements, or situations that are defined by nonexecutable statements. For example, words may be in the form: LET, READ, DATA, or PRINT.

Table C-3 shows the words defined by BASIC which specify executable statements.

Table C-3. Executable Words in BASIC

WORD	FUNCTION
LET	Compute and assign
GO TO	Transfer
IF, THEN	Test
FOR, NEXT, STEP	Loop
READ	Assign DATA variables
INPUT	Enter data in program
PRINT	Output
GO SUB, RETURN	Subroutine transfer
STOP	Terminate processing
MAT	Perform indicated matrix command

The LET statements are in the form

LET a = b

where a is a variable name and b is any valid expression or numeric constant. The LET statement signals that the expression b is to be evaluated and its value assigned to a.

The GO TO statements are in the form

GO TO x

where x is a line number. The command causes control to be transferred to the statement with the line number x.

The IF statements are in the form

IF r (relational operator) s THEN x

where r and s are expressions, variables, or numeric quantities, and x is a line number. This statement is executed in the following manner:

1. r and s are evaluated according to the relational operator specified.

2. If the value of r is in the specified relationship to the value of s, control is transferred to the statement numbered x.

3. If the value of r is not in the specified relationship to the value of

s, control is passed to the next sequential statement.

Loop processing commands are in the form

FOR a = b TO c STEP d

where *a* (a variable) is the index of *b* (the loop). An expression, variable, or numeric quantity is calculated to determine the initial value of *a*; *c* is the final value *a* may take before processing of the loop is terminated; and *d* is the step size taken in calculating *a*. Statements in the range of the loop include all those physically following the FOR statement up to the one immediately preceding the NEXT statement. They will be repeated until the terminal conditions for processing, as determined by the values of *a* and *c*, are met. If the STEP part of the command is omitted, *a* is increased by 1 on each pass through the loop.

The READ command is in the form

READ (list)

where (list) is a series of variable names separated by commas. The READ assigns the next values available in the DATA statement to the variables specified in the list. There will be as many values of data in the DATA statement assigned as there are elements in the list.

An INPUT command takes the form

INPUT (list)

where (list) is a series of variable names separated by commas, and INPUT requests the values of variables in its list to be specified at the remote terminal during program operation. There will be as many values requested at the terminal as there are elements in the list.

The PRINT command is in the form

PRINT (list)

where (list) is a series of variable names or alphabetic characters enclosed in quotes. These items are separated by commas. The numerical values of the variables in the list and the alphabetic quantities enclosed in punctuation at the remote terminal are displayed by PRINT.

A STOP command is in the form

STOP

This command causes program execution to terminate.

Matrix commands are in the form

MAT (Calculation)

where (Calculation) designates the operation to be performed. The BASIC system has been implemented with the facility to perform calculations on matrices of information without arithmetically programming the matrix operations. Matrix commands are signaled by the word MAT. With A, B, and C defined as matrices, these commands are illustrated and defined in Table C-4.

Table C-5 notes the definitions and functions of words that specify nonexecutable statements in BASIC.

Table C-4. Matrix Commands in BASIC

COMMAND	FUNCTION
MAT READ A	Read matrix A.
MAT PRINT A	Print matrix A.
MAT C = A + B	Add matrix A to matrix B and store in matrix C.
MAT C = A − B	Subtract matrix B from matrix A and store in matrix C.
MAT C = A * B	Multiply matrix A by matrix B and store in matrix C.
MAT C = INV (A)	Invert matrix A and store in matrix C.
MAT C = TRN (A)	Transpose matrix A and store in matrix C.
MAT C = x * A	Multiply matrix A by the number x and store in matrix C.
MAT C = ZER	Fill matrix C with zeros.
MAT C = CON	Fill matrix C with ones.
MAT C = IDN	Construct matrix C as the identity matrix.

Table C-5. Nonexecutable BASIC Words

WORD	FUNCTION
DATA	Provides data for READ list.
DEF	Defines user functions.
DIM	Allocates storage space for specified arrays.
END	Terminates program execution.
REM	Designates comment for program listing.
RESTORE	Reinitiates DATA values.

The DATA command is in the form

DATA (list)

where (list) is a series of numerical values (and sometimes alphabetic quantities enclosed in quotes) separated by commas, and DATA lists provide numeric values for variables occurring in a READ list. The DATA entries are referenced sequentially as READ statements are processed in the program.

A DIM statement is in the form

DIM (array names and sizes)

where (array names and sizes) designate which variables are to be allocated storage locations and how many each is to be allowed. Generally, DIM is not necessary if an array is a single.dimension with less than 11 elements or has two dimensions of a size less than 11 by 11. The BASIC system usually limits arrays to two dimensions.

The END command is in the form

END

This command terminates program execution, and it must be the last statement of the program physically.

A REM command is in the form

REM (comment)

where (comment) is information that is identification for the program and not part of the calculation. Usually, remarks are alphabetic in character.

The RESTORE command is in the form

RESTORE

It causes the next READ statement to reference the first element in the initial DATA statement of the program.

Several commonly used arithmetic and trigonometric functions are included in the BASIC language. It is not necessary to program the calculations for evaluating these functions, as the arithmetic is performed automatically upon presentation of the function name in the program. Table C-6 lists and defines the standard functions available. In addition to the functions defined by BASIC, a user may define his own program functions by using the DEF command. The command is in the form

DEF FNa (b) = r

where a is an alphabetic character that, with FN, names the function; b is a variable that appears in the program when the function is referenced; and r is an expression that defines the function calculation. During program execution, r is evaluated, using the value of b as it appears at each occurrence in the program.

The BASIC language can reference subprograms, or sequential lines of coding, which are repeated several times during program execution and are referenced from several locations in the program. The subprograms or subroutines are entered by the GOSUB command and left by the RETURN command.

The GOSUB command is in the form

GOSUB x

Table C-6. Standard BASIC Functions

FUNCTION	INTERPRETATION
SIN (N)	Sine n
COS (N)	Cosine n
TAN (N)	Tangent n
ATN (N)	Arc tangent n
EXP (N)	e^n
LOG (N)	Natural logarithm of n
ABS (N)	Absolute value of n
SQR (N)	Square root of n

where x is the line number of the first statement in the subroutine.

The RETURN commands are in the form

RETURN

These commands terminate processing of the subprogram and transfer control to the statement immediately following the GOSUB command that caused the subroutine reference.

EXTENSIONS TO BASIC

Most time-sharing services have implemented extensions to the BASIC language as it is described in this Appendix. Some of these additions, such as string capabilities, are becoming standard offerings in the language, since many compilers contain these features. The general characteristics of the more widespread extensions will be described in this section. Other less popular implementations will only be highlighted.

Many time-sharing systems allow more than one BASIC statement to be entered on a single physical line printed at a terminal. A punctuation symbol, such as a semicolon, is generally used as the delineator between the BASIC statements.

The number of characters in each BASIC statement is also subject to certain restrictions. Limitation to a 72 or 80 character statement (as restricted by the standard Teletype Model 33 printed line length) has been extended by some systems to include up to 255 characters per BASIC statement for other model terminals or continuation lines for the terminals with shorter printed lines.

Alphanumeric string capabilities have been implemented to some extent for nearly all BASIC compilers. This allows variables to be evaluated as an alphanumeric group of characters. In most cases, string variables are named by a single alphabetic character followed by an "S," while string contents are delimited by quotes. For example, LET CS = 'THIS IS A STRING' is a typical string assignment statement.

The READ, PRINT, INPUT, and DATA statements also contain strings of characters on many systems. This allows alphabetic information to be transferred via the program. For example, output information may be identified for printing by use of a string variable in a PRINT command. A further implementation of string capabilities (not currently prevalent) is string comparison. String variables are used, in this case, as conditions for the IF-THEN command.

Although it is not generally available, some BASIC systems allow definition of double precision, complex, or logical variables in a manner similar to FORTRAN IV.

Most systems do not supply extensions to the arithmetic and relational operators in BASIC. Sometimes, however, alternative symbols for the standard operators and quantitative operators, such as "much greater than" or "much less than," are available.

The word LET is optional for nearly all BASIC systems; thus, LET X = Y is equivalent to $X = Y$. Some systems allow multiple assignment of variables in a single statement. In this form LET X = 0, LET Y = 0, and LET Z = 0 may be condensed to LET X = Y = Z = 0. Another, less popular form of the multiple assignment command is the form LET X, Y, Z = 0.

Extensions to the GO TO command are provided on some systems. Statement transfer as a result of execution of the command may be determined by a computation that specifies one of several alternate statement numbers rather than a single one for GO TO transfer.

Extensions to the IF-THEN command allow the use of string variables as conditions for testing on some systems. Additionally, modifications that allow conditions to be imposed upon the THEN alternatives are occasionally implemented.

Many time-sharing systems allow access to data stored in files on on-line storage devices, such as disk memory. As implemented on these systems, BASIC contains commands that perform the reading and printing functions for file information. Some systems also have end-of-file tests and backspace commands for data manipulation.

Although BASIC as originated does not contain facilities for formatting data, various forms of output control have been implemented as language extensions. A TAB function is available on many systems to determine placement of blank spaces between data items on output. Some services have implemented picture type formatting in a fashion analogous to the FORMAT statement in FORTRAN. Number form and text may be specified for information printed with these commands.

Time-sharing services occasionally implement additional intrinsic functions for reference in the BASIC language. A random-number generator, an integral part function, and a sign function are often presented. Cotangent, secant, and cosecant, and hyperbolic trigonometric functions are sometimes available.

On some systems, internally set constants are considered part of the BASIC number system and are referenced by name. Pi, equaling 3.14159 . . . , is often preset and recognized by BASIC compilers.

Chaining functions are sometimes extended BASIC commands. Execution of these commands initiates system processes, which cause one group of program statements to replace another set in active machine memory. This allows execution of part of a program and replacement of that part by new program statements. Programs that are larger than the core memory available may be run in this manner.

APPENDIX D: FOCAL

FOCAL is a highly interactive programming language that, while powerful, occupies relatively little space in computer memory.* It is an interpretive language and was originally developed on and for PDP-8 computers. There are presently Digital Equipment versions of FOCAL available for PDP-8, PDP-11, PDP-12, and PDP-15 computers, as well as for many of Digital's traditional products (that is, computers once manufactured by Digital, but no longer manufactured). A nonsupported version of FOCAL is available for the DEC system-10 large computer line. Syntactically, all these versions are identical, but the error diagnostic messages vary from machine family to machine family.

The FOCAL language can be used in a minimum-configuration computer (4K words of memory and a teletypewriter), though extensions and program patches permit 8K versions and time-sharing versions of FOCAL to be employed. Originally introduced in late 1968, FOCAL has become so popular that there are an estimated 13,000 users of the language in the world today. In addition to an English language version, a German language version has been recently introduced.

The language is highly useful in mathematical problem solving, since its power can be utilized effectively in even minimum configurations. A PDP-11/20 with 4K of memory, for example, can invert a 10 × 10 matrix in 60 seconds.

---

*EDITOR'S NOTE: Appendix D. FOCAL was written by Stephen A. Kallis, Jr. FOCAL is a registered trademark of Digital Equipment Corporation.

OVERVIEW

The FOCAL language can operate either directly, in the command mode, or indirectly, following program instructions. The same instructions are used in either case, but in the command mode, only one line of instructions is executed at a time.

Twelve commands are all that are necessary to use FOCAL, either directly or indirectly, to write programs (see Table D-1):

1. TYPE: Used to print text, results of calculations, and values of variables.
2. ASK: Used to assign values of variables from the keyboard (indirect mode only).
3. SET: Used to define variables and evaluate expressions.
4. GO or GOTO: GO is used to initiate a program; GOTO is used to direct program control to a specific line number.
5. IF: Used to transfer program control conditionally after a comparison (indirect mode only).
6. DO: Used to execute a specific line or group of lines (indirect mode only).
7. RETURN: Used to terminate DO routines.
8. QUIT: Used to halt program execution, returning control to the user.
9. FOR: Used to increment a number and to execute a user-specified command for each value of the number incremented.
10. COMMENT or CONTINUE: Used for nonexecutable program steps.
11. ERASE or ERASE ALL: Used to erase part of a program (ERASE) or an entire program (ERASE ALL).
12. MODIFY: Used to edit words or characters on a program line.

Because the first letter of each command is different, commands can be abbreviated, to save space and input time.

Values to user-defined variables, either in the command mode or as part of a program, can be assigned by FOCAL. The variables consist of one or two characters. The first character must be alphabetic, though the letter F cannot be used because it is reserved for function names, as will be explained later. Although the user may define variable names with more than two characters, FOCAL recognizes only the first two characters; hence, these characters must be unique.

Variables are assigned by the SET command. In command mode, examples might be:

```
*SET A = 82326            *SET C9 = 177.6
*SET B = 777442           *SET PI = 3.14159
*SET C1 = 19.84           *SET RATE = 12.5
```

Variables may also be subscripted.

Table D-1. FOCAL Command Summary

COMMAND	ABBREVIATION	EXAMPLE OF FORM	EXPLANATION
ASK	A	ASK X, Y, Z	FOCAL types a colon for each variable; the user types a value to define each variable.
COMMENT	C	COMMENT	If a line begins with the letter C, the remainder of the line will be ignored.
CONTINUE	C	C	Dummy lines.
DO	D	DO 4.1	Execute line 4.1; return to command following DO command.
ERASE	E	ERASE	Erases the symbol table.
		ERASE 2.0	Erases all group 2 lines.
		ERASE 2.1	Deletes line 2.1.
		ERASE ALL	Deletes all user input.
FOR	F	For I x, y, z (commands) *or* FOR i, x, z, (commands)	Where the command following is executed at each new value. x = initial value of i. y = value added to i until i is greater than z.
GO	G	GO	Starts indirect program at lowest numbered line number.
GO?	G?	GO?	Starts at lowest numbered line number and traces entire indirect program until another ? is encountered, until an error is encountered, or until completion of program.
GOTO	G	GOTO 3.4	Starts indirect program (transfers control to line 3.4.) Must have argument.
IF	I	IF (X) Ln, Ln, Ln or IF (X) Ln, Ln; (commands) *or* IF (X) Ln; (commands)	Where X is a defined identifier, a value, or an expression, followed by one to three line numbers. If X is less than zero, control is transferred to the first line number; if X is equal to zero, control is to the second line number; and if X is greater than zero, control passes to the third line number.
LIBRARY CALL	L C	LIBRARY CALL name	Calls stored program from the disk.

142   *Auerbach on Minicomputers*

Table D-1. (Continued)

COMMAND	ABBREVIATION	EXAMPLE OF FORM	EXPLANATION
LIBRARY DELETE	L D	LIBRARY DELETE name	Removes program from the disk.
LIBRARY LIST	L L	LIBRARY LIST	Types directory of stored program names.
LIBRARY SAVE	L S	LIBRARY SAVE	Saves program on the disk.
LINK	L	L	For disk monitor system; FOCAL types four locations, indicating start and end of text area, end of variable list, and bottom of pushdown list.
LOCATIONS	L	L	For paper tape system; types same locations as LINK.
MODIFY	M	MODIFY 1.15	Enables editing of any character on line 1.15.
QUIT	Q	QUIT	Return control to the user.
RETURN	R	RETURN	Terminates DO subroutines; returning to the original sequence.
SET	S	SET A = 5/B*C	Defines identifiers in the symbol table.
TYPE	T	TYPE A+B–C;	Evaluates expression and types = and result in current output format.
		TYPE A–C, C/E;	Computes and types each expression separated by commas.
		TYPE "TEXT STRING"	Types text. May be followed by ! to generate carriage return-line feed, or by # to generate carriage return.
WRITE	W	WRITE / WRITE ALL	FOCAL types out the entire indirect program.
		WRITE 1.0	FOCAL types out all group 1 lines.
		WRITE 1.1	FOCAL types out line 1.1.

OPERATIONS

Table D-2 lists FOCAL operators and reserved symbols. To print the results of arithmetic or other defined operations, the TYPE command is used.

Table D-2. FOCAL Operators and Reserved Symbols

Mathematical Operators
- ↑ Exponentiation
- * Multiplication
- / Division
- + Addition
- − Subtraction

Control Characters
- % Output format delimiter
- ! Carriage return and line feed
- # Carriage return
- $ Type symbol table contents
- ( ) Parentheses
- [ ] Square brackets (mathematics)
- < > Angle brackets
- " " Quotation marks (text string)
- ? ? Question marks (trace feature)
- * Asterisk (high-speed reader input)

Terminators
SPACE key (names)
RETURN key (lines)
ALT MODE key (with ASK statement)
Comma (expression)
Semicolon (compounds and statements)

For arithmetic operations, standard symbols are used:

- + addition (last priority)
- − subtraction (last priority)
- / division (third priority)
- * multiplication (second priority)
- ↑ exponentiation (highest priority)

Thus, in the command mode, the command "TYPE 3/4" followed by depressing the carriage return key produces "= 0.7500" followed by an asterisk; the asterisk indicates that the command mode is available for further action. Normally, FOCAL prints out answers to four decimal places, though the user can alter this by different techniques. Parenthetical expressions are allowed, and such expressions can even be nested, such as: *TYPE (1 + (1/2047)) ↑ 2047. Unless otherwise provided for by the user, FOCAL calculations are accurate to six significant figures.

The TYPE command is also used to generate character strings, but such strings must be enclosed in quotation marks ("). Thus, TYPE "MARY HAD A LITTLE LAMB" followed by striking the carriage return key produces the message within the quotes. This feature is almost invariably reserved for programs rather than for operations in the command mode.

Variables, text, and arithmetic operations may be included in an operation. Thus,

    *SET N = 5∅
    *TYPE "M IS", N/2

would result in:

    M IS = 25.∅∅∅∅*

Any variable, constant, or expression in a TYPE (or ASK) command must be followed by a comma, a semicolon, or a carriage return.

The ASK command is normally used in indirect commands to permit the user to define numerical values of variables for a program run, though it can be used in the command mode:

    *ASK X

followed by a carriage return produces a colon (:), after which the user can enter a numerical entry:

    :25

The value is assigned to the variable only when the user types a terminator (comma, semicolon, or carriage return); so, he can change his entry at any time prior to typing the terminator. He does this by typing a back arrow (← or SHIFT/0) immediately after the value and before typing the terminator; thus,

    *ASK X
    :27 33

Multiple values can be asked:

    *ASK X, Y, Z
    :22
    :33
    :45

Being assigned variables, these values can be recalled from memory:

*TYPE X, Y, Z

= 22.0000 = 33.0000 = 45.0000

As with TYPE commands, text output can be used with an ASK command:

*ASK "WHAT IS YOUR AGE?" AG

WHAT IS YOUR AGE? :33

In this case, AG is the variable.

Semicolons permit more than one instruction or command to be written in a single line:

*TYPE (2*3)↑2; TYPE 4/9; TYPE 11+7; ASK AGE

results in

= 36.0000 = 0.4444 = 18.0000:

Such multiple commands can be made less confusing by doing a line feed and carriage return between each operation's output. The exclamation point (!), which is a command character, is used for this purpose. Thus, in our example,

*TYPE (2*2)↑2, !; TYPE 4/9 !; TYPE 11+7, !; ASK AGE

results in

= 36.0000

= 0.4444

= 18.0000

PROGRAMS AND CONTROL COMMANDS

Programs in FOCAL use numbered lines, though more than one command can be entered on each line. Line numbers run from 1.01 to some upper limit that is determined in part by the version of FOCAL being used. Line numbers cannot include integer numbers. It is not necessary to use every potential line number. A simple FOCAL program might be:

*1.1 ASK "HOW MANY APPLES DOES BILL HAVE?" BA

*1.2 ASK "HOW MANY APPLES DOES JOHN HAVE?" JA

*1.3 ASK "HOW MANY APPLES DOES MARY HAVE?" MA

*1.4 TYPE "THEY ALL TOGETHER HAVE" BA+JA+MA,
      "APPLES!"!

To run such a program, the user types GO and hits the carriage return key. The program lists the questions, accepts user input, and presents the result:

*GO

HOW MANY APPLES DOES BILL HAVE? :1∅

HOW MANY APPLES DOES JOHN HAVE? :2∅

HOW MANY APPLES DOES MARY HAVE? :3∅

THEY ALL TOGETHER HAVE 6∅ APPLES!

   *

Normally, a program terminates when it executes the final line of the program, but the QUIT command can be used as an end or stop statement. When the QUIT command is executed, an asterisk is printed and the computer returns to the command mode.

Related to the GO command is the GOTO command. This directs the program to start at a specified line number. Thus, if in our previous program the user had typed GOTO 1.2, the program would start at the second line, omitting the first question. A program can be made totally repetitious by making the last instruction a GOTO statement to the first line number.

The FOCAL statement for conditional decisions is the IF statement. It is generally used to compare one or more variables to a given condition. The quantity or quantities to be compared are enclosed in parentheses. The statement

*2.1 IF (X–Y)3.1,4.1,5.1

evaluates the mathematical expression subtracting Y from X. If the result is a negative value, the program transfers control to line 3.1. If the result is zero, the control is transferred to line 4.1; a positive result transfers control to line 5.1. Thus, a simple program for comparing two numbers might be

*1.1 ASK "X?", X
*1.2 ASK "Y?" Y
*2.1 IF (X–Y)3.1,4.1,5.1
*3.1 TYPE "Y IS THE LARGER NUMBER"!; QUIT
*4.1 TYPE "BOTH NUMBERS ARE EQUAL"!; QUIT
*5.1 TYPE "X IS THE LARGER NUMBER"!

Without the QUIT, all three statements would be printed if Y were larger. If previous elements of the program continue beyond line 5.1, a QUIT command is necessary if that is to be the last statement.

The COMMAND or CONTINUE command permits the entry of a dummy line; a COMMENT can be used in the command mode, too. This feature is particularly useful in situations where information to a user is added to the beginning of a paper tape when a FOCAL program is being loaded into the computer.

The ERASE command permits all or part of the program to be eliminated. When a user wishes to eliminate a line, he types the command and the line number; thus,

    *ERASE 3.11

Were the user to type "ERASE 3," the whole section of the program, including any and all lines from 3.01 to 3.99, is erased. If the user wishes to eliminate the program, he types ERASE ALL.

The DO command directs that a specific line or group of lines be executed. The command

    *DO 5.1

directs that only a specific line be executed. The command

    *DO 5

directs that all lines in group 5 be executed. Related to the DO command is the RETURN command, which is used to terminate DO routines. Using DO and RETURN commands shortens program length. For instance, we could rewrite our "apples" program thus:

    *1.1 DO 4.1; ASK "BILL HAVE?" BA
    *1.2 DO 4.1; ASK "JOHN HAVE?" JA
    *1.3 DO 4.1; ASK "MARY HAVE?" MA
    *1.4 TYPE "THEY ALL TOGETHER HAVE" BA+JA+MA,"
          APPLES!"!;QUIT
    *4.1 TYPE "HOW MANY APPLES DOES "; RETURN

In operation, this program will perform identically to the simple version.

In addition to ERASE, there are other editing commands. The WRITE command is used to print a listing of the program or of its individual elements. Thus, if the user wishes to list a line, he writes

    *WRITE 1.2

If he wants the whole section listed, he writes

    *WRITE 1

If the user requires a listing of the whole program, he writes

*WRITE ALL

The WRITE ALL command can be used in conjunction with the paper tape punch on a Teletype terminal, or equivalent, to permit a paper tape version of the program to be made.

Another editing command is MODIFY. This command permits the user to alter one or more characters in a line. Consider the line

*3.45 SET Y = M*Y+C

If the user wishes to change the formula to *Y=MX+B*, he types

*MODIFY 3.45

The response after the carriage return is a pause until the user types in the first character to be modified, in this case, *Y*.

The computer does not echo the character. It types the line to the character in question, and pauses:

SET Y

Because the first *Y* is not to be altered, the user simultaneously depresses the CONTROL and the L keys. This signals the computer to continue until encountering the character again:

SET Y = M*Y

To delete a character, the RUBOUT key on the keyboard should be hit; FOCAL acknowledges a rubout with a backslash. Thus,

SET Y = M*Y \ X

To cause the computer to search for a different character in the line, the CONTROL and the G keys are struck; a bell sounds, the new character is entered by striking its key (in this case C), and the line continues to print out from that point. Because the line is picked up at the point of the last correction, characters already printed on the paper cannot be "found":

SET Y = M*Y\X+C\B

When the RETURN key is hit, the modified line is complete.

When text editing is done, the values in the user's symbol table are reset to zero. Therefore, if the user defines the symbols in direct statements and then uses a MODIFY command, he must redefine them. If the symbols, however, are defined indirectly (that is, within the program), they are not affected.

Error Signals and Trace Feature

When an erroneous command is encountered (such as dividing by zero), FOCAL generates an error message and returns to the command mode. The precise messages vary among different versions of FOCAL. Table D-3 lists the PDP-8 FOCAL error messages. When an error is encountered in a pro-

Table D-3. FOCAL Error Diagnostics, PDP-8 Version*

CODE	MEANING
?00.00	Manual start given from console.
?01.00	Interrupt from keyboard via CTRL/C.
?01.40	Illegal step or line number used.
?01.78	Group number is too large.
?01.96	Double periods found in a line number.
?01.:5	Line number is too large.
?01.;4	Group zero is an illegal line number.
?02.32	Nonexistent group referenced by 'DO'.
?02.52	Nonexistent line referenced by 'DO'.
?02.79	Storage was filled by pushdown list.
?03.05	Nonexistent line was used after 'GOTO' or 'IF'.
?03.28	Illegal command used.
?04.39	Left of "=" in error in 'FOR' or 'SET'.
?04.52	Excess right terminators encountered.
?04.60	Illegal terminator in 'FOR' command.
?04.:3	Missing argument in display command.
?05.48	Bad argument to 'MODIFY'.
?06.06	Illegal use of function or number.
?06.54	Storage is filled by variables.
?07.22	Operator missing in expression or double 'E'.
?07.38	No operator used before parenthesis.
?07.:9	No argument given after function call.
?07.;6	Illegal function name or double operators.
?08.47	Parentheses do not match.
?09.11	Bad argument in 'ERASE'.
?10.:5	Storage was filled by text.
?11.35	Input buffer has overflowed.
?20.34	Logarithm of zero requested.
?23.36	Literal number is too large.
?26.99	Exponent is too large or negative.
?28.73	Division by zero requested.
?30.05	Imaginary square roots requred.
?31.<7	Illegal character, unavailable command, or unavailable function used.

*For FOCAL, 1969 only.

gram, FOCAL prints out the error message and identifies the line in which it occurred. Thus, a program that was interrupted by an error might print:

   ?09.11 @ 2.2

which, in PDP-8 FOCAL means that the open and close parentheses at line 2.2 did not match. This enables the user to input "WRITE 2.2" so that the line can be examined.

   Another feature is trace. By typing a question mark before the GO command, the program traces its operations while running:

   *?GO

If there are no anomalies in the program, it runs to termination. The trace feature can also be used to type out sections of a program. In the indirect mode, FOCAL prints all characters between two question marks. Thus,

   *1.1 SET A=1; SET B=2; SET C=3
   *1.2 TYPE ? A+B—C?

prints the following when run:

   *GO
   A+B—C = Ø.ØØØØ*

FOCAL FUNCTIONS

   FOCAL has standard functions such as square root to increase the flexibility and scope of the language (see Table D-4). On some versions of FOCAL, a number of these functions are optional and may be deleted during the initial dialogue. These functions must be used with a legal FOCAL command; they cannot be used as commands by themselves. All these functions use four-character designators plus parentheses, and all begin with the letter F.

   The sine function FSIN expresses the sine of a user-specified angle in radians. The format for FSIN is

   FSIN (angle). Thus,
   *TYPE FSIN(3.14159/4)
   = Ø.7Ø71*

The format for calculating the sine of an angle in degrees is

   FSIN(degrees*3.14159/180)
      *TYPE FSIN(3Ø*3.14159/18Ø)
      = Ø.5ØØØ*

The cosine function FCOS operates in the same manner.

Trigonometric functions may be combined to calculate other functions via normal rules of trigonometry.

The exponential function FEXP computes $e(e = 2.71828 \ldots)$ to a power specified by the user. Its format is

FEXP(power)

   *TYPE FEXP(1)

   = 2.71823*

The logarithmic function FLOG finds the natural logarithm of a number. Its format is

FLOG(number)

   *TYPE FLOG(2.71828)

   = Ø.9999*

The arctangent function FATN calculates the angle in radians of a user-specified tangent. Its format is

FATN(tangent)

   *TYPE FATN(1.)

   = Ø.7854

The square root function computes the square root of an expression. Its format is

FSQT(expression)

   *TYPE FSQT(9)

   = 3.ØØØØ

   *SET Q = 12; TYPE FSQT(Q)

   = 3.4641*

The sign part function FSGN outputs the sign (that is, + or −) of a number (expressed by zero or number 1). The format for FSGN is

FSGN(expression)

   *TYPE FSGN(6–4)

   = 1.ØØØØ*

   *TYPE FSGN(Ø)

   = 1.ØØØØ*

   *TYPE FSGN(2–5)

   = 01.ØØØØ*

Table D-4. FOCAL Functions

CALL	FUNCTION
FSQT ( )	Square root
FABS ( )	Absolute value
FSGN ( )	Sign part of the expression
FITR ( )	Integer part of the expression
FRAN ( )	A random number generator
FEXP ( )	Natural base to the power
FSIN ( )	Sine
FCOS ( )	Cosine
FATN ( )	Arctangent
FLOG ( )	Naperian log
FDIS ( )	Scope functions
FADC ( )	Analog-to-digital input function
FNEW ( )	User function
FCOM ( )	Storage function

The integer part function FITR outputs the integer part of a number. Its format is

FITR(expression)
   *TYPE FITR(3.3336)
   = 3.0000*
   *SET X=3.1412;TYPE (X–FITR(X))
   = 0.1412*

The random number function FRAN generates pseudo-random numbers. In some versions of FOCAL, this is restricted over a range, producing some bias. Its format is

FRAN( )
   *TYPE FRAN( )
   = 0.7724

The random number generated is always less than 1, and FRAN routines with inherent biases (the PDP-8 FOCAL FRAN function ranges between 0.50000 and 0.9999) can produce a less biased result by a short program:

   *SET A-FRAN( )*50
   *SET B=A–FITR(A)
   *TYPE B
   = 0.3327*

FOCAL has a facility FNEW to handle user-defined functions coded in assembly language. The format of a user-defined function is

FNEW ( )

Many FOCAL functions can be nested. Thus, the fourth root of a number can be determined by FSQT(FSQT(number)), etc.

FLOATING POINT AND NUMERICAL FORMATS

FOCAL can print out results in a standard floating-point form if desired. The user obtains this by requesting

TYPE %, X

where X is the expression to be evaluated. For instance,

*TYPE %, 678

= $\emptyset$.678$\emptyset\emptyset\emptyset$E+$\emptyset$3*

where E is equal to 10, +03 is the exponent of 10 (that is, 10^3), making the expression equal to 0.678 times 10^3, or 678.

After floating point is requested, all answers are in that format until otherwise requested. Numbers can be printed in the usual decimal notation by the following format: TYPE %XX.xx, where XX designates the total number of figures in the result, and xx is a *two-digit* number representing the number of significant figures beyond the decimal point. Thus,

*TYPE %, FSQT(68)

= $\emptyset$.824621E+$\emptyset$1*

*TYPE %8.04,FSQT(68)

= 8.2462*

*TYPE %4.02,FSQT(68)

= 8.24*

*TYPE %4, FSQT(68)

= 8*

Closing Points

One feature of FOCAL shown in Table D-1 is that commands can be abbreviated and represented by single characters. Thus, SET can be represented by S; TYPE by T, etc. These single-character abbreviations save memory space, making even more compact programs.

In some versions of FOCAL, overlays are available for multiple use or library operations. These are configuration-dependent operations and thus are beyond the scope of this discussion.

APPENDIX E: FORTRAN

The FORTRAN (FORmula TRANslation) programming language was originally released by IBM early in 1957. Although the initial version, designed for the IBM 704 computer, provided significant advantages over machine language programming, it was still machine-dependent. In June 1958, IBM released FORTRAN II, which contained extensions over the original 704 FORTRAN, such as subroutine capability (including common sharing of storage) and function definitions. Subsequently, IBM issued versions of FORTRAN for the 709, 650, 1620, 7070, and 7030 computers. The first non-IBM version of FORTRAN was introduced by UNIVAC for the Solid State 80 system in 1961. Other manufacturers followed suit, and soon each company had its own version of the language. The FORTRAN III, developed and implemented internally by IBM, featured the addition of Boolean operations. In 1962, FORTRAN IV was announced; this version contained major advancements and revisions of FORTRAN II, such as logical IF and TYPE statements (INTEGER, LOGICAL, REAL, etc.).

The impact of FORTRAN on the data processing community was reflected in the wide acceptance by computer manufacturers and even more so in its reception by the scientific community. Through its relatively simple rules of syntax, FORTRAN eliminated the need for scientists and engineers to use a programmer as an intermediary. As the use of the language spread, the variations became more pronounced, until May 1962, when the American Standards Association (which became the United States of America Standards Institute, USASI, and is now the American National Standards Institute, ANSI) formed a committee to develop an American Standard FORTRAN.

155

Two standards were eventually produced: Basic FORTRAN (nearly equivalent to FORTRAN II) and FORTRAN (similar to FORTRAN IV). Since Basic FORTRAN is a proper subset of FORTRAN, the following discussion of language will start with a description of the features of ANSI FORTRAN, followed by a discussion of the Basic FORTRAN exceptions.

FEATURES OF ANSI FORTRAN

Some of the terms and concepts used in this discussion are defined below.

Program unit: Consists of statements and comments. Statements are composed of lines; the first line of a statement is called the "initial" line, and all subsequent lines are called "continuation" lines. Comments are lines that are not statements and are used to provide information to the programmer.

Statements: May be "executable" (specify the action of the program) or "nonexecutable" (describe the use of the program, the characteristics of the operands, editing information, statement functions, or data management).

Executable programs: Those that can be used as self-contained computing procedures and may contain both executable and nonexecutable statements.

Main program: A set of statements and comments not containing a FUNCTION or SUBROUTINE statement.

Procedure subprogram: Sometimes referred to simply as a subprogram; a self-contained computing procedure headed by a FUNCTION or SUBROUTINE statement.

Function subprogram: An external procedure that is defined by FORTRAN statements headed by a FUNCTION statement.

Subroutine subprogram: An external procedure defined by FORTRAN statements headed by a SUBROUTINE statement.

Names: Used to reference objects such as data or procedures.

Operators: Used to specify action upon named objects.

Features of FORTRAN are presented in seven categories: program form, data types, data and procedure identification, expressions, statements, procedures and subprograms, and programs. Note that not all of the features outlined here are included in ANSI Basic FORTRAN. Exceptions are discussed in the succeeding section.

Program Form

Program units are composed of characters grouped into lines and statements. The ANSI FORTRAN character set includes all alphabetic characters and the digits 0 through 9 in addition to the special characters listed in Table E-1. In addition to the decimal digits 0 to 9, FORTRAN supports, in the PAUSE and STOP statements, the octal digits 0 to 7.

Table E-1. ANSI FORTRAN Special Character Set

CHARACTER	NAME OF CHARACTER
	Blank
=	Equals
+	Plus
–	Minus
*	Asterisk
/	Slash
(	Left parenthesis
)	Right parenthesis
,	Comma
.	Decimal point
$	Dollar sign

Program units include:

Comment lines: Provide information to the user and are not executed as part of the program. They are indicated by a C in column 1. Note that comment lines do not affect the program in any way.

End lines: Indicate the end of the program unit. Every program unit must physically terminate with an end line. End lines are blank in columns 1 through 6, and have the characters E, N, and D, in that order, in columns 7 to 72, with as many blanks as desired preceding or interspersed with these characters.

Initial lines: These are neither comment nor end lines and contain the character 0 or blank in column 6.

Continuation lines: These are neither comment nor end lines and contain digits other than 0 or blank in column 6.

Statements: Consist of an initial line optionally followed by up to 19 ordered continuation lines. They are written in columns 7 through 72 of the initial and continuation lines.

Statement labels: Provide a label for statements to be referred to in other statements. Statement labels are integers from 1-99999 written in columns 1 to 5 and are unique within a program. Leading zeros are ignored.

Symbolic names: Provide a method of distinguishing variables. They contain from 1 to 6 alphanumeric characters, the first of which must be alphabetic.

Data Types

Six different types of data are defined: integer, real, double precision, complex, logical, and Hollerith. Data type association is defined by the symbolic name by declaration in a type statement for all but Hollerith types. A type-statement association overrides implied associations such as that for integer and real.

Integer type data: Always an exact representation of an integer value, and may assume positive, negative, or zero values. It may only assume integral values.

Real type data: A processor approximation to the value of a real number. It may assume positive, negative, and zero values.

Double precision type data: Similar to real type with the exception that the degree of approximation is greater for double precision.

Complex type data: A processor approximation to the value of a complex number. Representation of the approximation is in the form of an ordered pair of real data. The first of the pair represents the real part and the second the imaginary part.

Logical type data: Assume only the truth values of true or false.

Hollerith type data: A string of characters, which may consist of any characters capable of representation in the processor.

Data and Procedure Identification

Constants, variables, and arrays are identified by data names. Constants are always defined during execution and may not be redefined.

Integer constants: Written as nonempty strings of digits. The constant is the digit string interpreted as a decimal.

Real constants: Written as an integer part, decimal point, and decimal part. A decimal exponent is written as the letter E followed by an integer constant.

Double precision constants: Written as a real constant followed by a double precision exponent (a double precision exponent is written with the letter D followed by an integer constant).

Complex constants: Written as ordered pairs of real constants separated by commas and enclosed within parentheses.

Logical constants: Written TRUE and FALSE.

Hollerith constant: Written as an integer constant n followed by the letter H followed by any n characters capable of representation by the processor. Hollerith constants may be written only in the argument list of a CALL statement and in the data initialization statement.

Variable: Data identified by a symbolic name. Such data may be referenced and defined.

Array: An ordered set of data of one, two, or three dimensions identified by a symbolic name.

Array element: One of the members of the set of data of an array identified by the subscript, which points out the particular element of the array.

Subscript: Written as a parenthesized list of subscript expressions separated by commas. The number of subscript expressions must correspond to the declared dimensionality.

Subscript expression: Written as one of the following: $c*v + k$, $c*v - k$, $c*v$, $v + k$, $v - k$, v, k, where c and k are integer constants and v is an integer variable reference.

Procedures: Identified by symbolic names. These are statement functions, intrinsic functions, external functions, or external subroutines.

Type of a constant: Determined by the first character of its name in the absence of an explicit declaration. Constants with either I, J, K, L, M, or N as the first character are integer types and any other letter implies real type. An array element has the same type as its array name.

Dummy arguments: Identify variables, arrays, subroutines, or external functions.

Expressions

An arithmetic expression is formed with arithmetic operators and arithmetic elements. Arithmetic operators are defined in Table E-2. Relational expressions consist of two arithmetic expressions separated by a relational operator and will have the value true or false as the relation is true or false. Relational operators are presented in Table E-3.

Table E-2. FORTRAN Arithmetic Operators

OPERATOR	FUNCTION
+	Addition, positive value (zero + element)
−	Subtraction, negative value (zero − element)
*	Multiplication
/	Division
**	Exponentiation

Table E-3. FORTRAN Relational Operators

OPERATOR	FUNCTION
.LT.	Less than
.LE.	Less than or equal to
.EQ.	Equal to
.NE.	Not equal to
.GT.	Greater than
.GE.	Greater than or equal to

Logical expressions are formed with logical operators and logical elements and have the value TRUE or FALSE. Logical operators appear in Table E-4.

Table E-4. FORTRAN Logical Operators

OPERATOR	LOGICAL FUNCTION
.OR.	Disjunction
.AND.	Conjunction
.NOT.	Negation

Statements

Program statements may be classified as executable or nonexecutable. Executable statements specify actions; nonexecutable statements describe the characteristics and arrangement of data, editing information, statement functions, and classification of program units.

Executable statements are of three types: assignment statements, control statements, and input/output statements.

Assignment statements are defined as arithmetic, logical, and GO TO. Arithmetic assignment statements are in the form

   v = e

where *v* is a variable name and *e* is an arithmetic expression. Execution of this statement evaluates the expression *e* and alters the variable *v*. Logical assignment statements are in the form

   v = e

where *v* is a variable name or a logical array element name and *e* is a logical expression. Execution of this statement evaluates the logical expression and assigns its value to the logical entity. The GO TO assignment statements are in the form

   ASSIGN k TO i

where *k* is a statement label and *i* is an integer variable. Execution of this statement causes subsequent execution of any assigned GO TO statement using that integer variable to branch to that statement label. The statement label must refer to an executable statement in the same program unit in which the ASSIGN statement appears. Once mentioned in an ASSIGN statement, an integer variable may not be referenced in any statement other than an assigned GO TO statement until it has been redefined.

Control statements are of eight types:

1. GO TO statements.
2. Arithmetic IF statement.
3. Logical IF statement.
4. CALL statement.
5. RETURN statement.
6. CONTINUE statement.
7. Program control statements.
8. DO statement.

Statement labels used in control statements must be associated with executable statements within the same program unit in which the control statement apepars.

The GO TO statements are of three types: unconditional GO TO, assigned GO TO, computed GO TO. Unconditional GO TO statements are in the form

   GO TO k

where k is a statement label. Execution of this statement causes the statement identified by the statement label to be executed next. Assigned GO TO statements are in the form

GO TO i, $(k_1, k_2, \ldots k_n)$

where i is an integer variable reference and the ks are statement labels. Execution of an assigned GO TO statement causes the statement identified by the statement label in the parenthesized list referenced by i to be executed. The current value of i must have been assigned by the previous execution of an ASSIGN statement. Computed GO TO statements are in the form

GO TO $(k_1, k_2 \ldots k_n)$, i

where the ks are statement labels and the i is an integer variable reference. Execution of this statement causes the statement identified by the statement label k to be executed next.

Arithmetic IF statements are in the form

IF $(e)k_1, k_2, k_3$

where e is any arithmetic expression of type integer, real or double precision, and the ks are statement labels. Execution of this statement causes evaluation of the expression e, following which the statement identified by the statement label k_1, k_2, or k_3 is executed next as the value of e is less than zero, zero, or greater than zero, respectively.

Logical IF statements are in the form

IF (e) S

where e is a logical expression and S is any executable statement except a DO statement or another logical IF statement. Execution of this statement causes evaluation of the expression e; also, if e is false, statement S is treated as a CONTINUE statement, and if e is true, statement S is executed.

The CALL statements are in the forms

CALL s $(a_1, a_2, \ldots a_n)$
CALL s

where s is the name of a subroutine and the as are actual arguments. Execution of this statement references the designated subroutine.

The RETURN statements are in the form

RETURN

Execution of this statement when it appears in a subroutine subprogram causes return of control to the current calling program unit.

The CONTINUE statements are in the form

> CONTINUE

Execution of this statement causes continuation of the normal execution sequence.

Two types of program control statements, STOP and PAUSE, are provided; STOP statements are in the form

> STOP n
> STOP

where n is an octal digit string of length from one to five. Execution of this statement terminates the executable program. The PAUSE statements are in the form

> PAUSE n
> PAUSE

where n is an octal digit string with a length from one to five. Execution of this statement causes a cessation of the executable program. Execution is resumable, with the decision to resume under user control.

The DO statements are in the form

> DO n i = m_1, m_2, m_3
> DO n i = m_1, m_2

where n is the statement label of an executable statement, i is an integer variable name (the control variable), m_1 is the initial parameter, m_2 is the terminal parameter, and m_3 is the increment. Execution of this statement causes the loop of program statements between the DO statement and statement n to be executed as the value of i goes from m_1 to m_2 in increments of m_3 (note that if m_3 is not specified in the DO statement, its value is assumed to be 1). If the range of a DO statement contains another DO statement, the latter must be a subset of the former (a DO is considered to be a subset of another if its entire range falls within the range of the containing DO). A DO statement is said to have an extended range if both of the following conditions apply:

1. There exists a GO TO or arithmetic IF statement within the range of the innermost DO of a completely nested nest that can cause control to pass out of that nest.

2. There exists a GO TO or arithmetic IF statement not within the nest that could be executed after a statement of the type described above, and the execution of which could cause control to return into the range of the

innermost DO of the completely nested nest.

If both conditions apply, the extended range is defined as the set of all executable statements that may be executed between all pairs of control statements, the first of which satisfies the condition of (1) and the second of (2). Note that a GO TO or an arithmetic IF statement may not pass control into the range of a DO unless it is being executed as part of the extended range of that particular DO.

Input/output statements are of two types: READ and WRITE statements and auxiliary input/output statements. The first type consists of the statements that cause transfer of records of sequential files to and from internal storage. The second type includes BACKSPACE and REWIND statements (which handle positioning of such an external file) along with ENDFILE (which handles demarcation of such an external file).

The READ statements may be formatted or unformatted. Formatted READ statements are in the form

    READ (u, f) k
    READ (u, f)

where u is the input unit, f is the format statement number, and k is a list. Execution of this statement causes the input of the next record from the unit identified by u. The information is then scanned and converted as specified by the format f. Resulting values are assigned to the elements specified by the list. Unformatted READ statements are in the form

    READ (u) k
    READ (u)

where u is the input unit and k is a list. Execution of this statement causes the input of the next record from the unit identified by u. The WRITE statements may be formatted or unformatted. Formatted WRITE statements are in the form

    WRITE (u, f) k
    WRITE (u, f)

where u is the output unit, f is the format statement, and k is a list. Execution of this statement creates the next records on the unit, identified by u, which are converted and positioned as specified by f. The unformatted WRITE statement is in the form

    WRITE (u) k

where u is the output unit and k is a list. Execution of this statement creates the next record on the unit, identified by u, of the sequence of values specified by the list. The BACKSPACE statement is in the form

    BACKSPACE u

where u is the input/output unit. Execution of this statement causes the position of the unit to be moved to change the immediately preceding record to the next record. A REWIND statement is in the form

    REWIND u

where u is the input/output unit. Execution of this statement causes the unit identified by u to be repositioned to its initial point. An ENDFILE statement is in the form

    ENDFILE u

where u is the input/output unit. Execution of this statement causes the recording of an ENDFILE record (signaling the demarcation of a sequential file) on the unit identified by u.

Printing of formatted records is possible through the use of carriage control characters in the first position of the record. The four carriage control characters are presented in Table E-5.

Table E-5. Carriage Control Characters

CHARACTER	VERTICAL SPACING BEFORE PRINTING
Blank	One line
0	Two lines
1	To first line of next page
+	No advance

Input/output lists specify the names of the variables and array elements to which values are assigned on input and specify the references to variables and array elements whose values are transmitted on output. An input/output list can be a simple list (a variable name, an array element name, an array name, or two simple lists separated by a comma), a simple list enclosed in parentheses, a DO-implied list (a simple list followed by a comma and a DO-implied specification), or two lists separated by a comma. The DO-implied specifications are in the form

    $i = m_1, m_2, m_3$

    $i = m_1, m_2$

where the elements i, m_1, m_2, m_3 are as defined for the DO statement.

Five types of nonexecutable statements are provided in ANSI FORTRAN.

1. Specification statements.
2. Data initialization statements.
3. FORMAT statement.
4. Function-defining statements.
5. Subprogram-defining statements.

Specification statements are of five types: DIMENSION, COMMON, EQUIVA-
LENCE, EXTERNAL, and type statements. Sizes and dimensions of arrays are
indicated through the array declarator in the form

   v (i)

where v (the declarator name) is a symbolic name and i (declarator subscript) is composed of one, two, or three expressions, each of which may
be an integer constant or an integer variable name. If any of the entries in
a declarator subscript is an integer variable name, the array is called an adjustable array, and the variable names are called adjustable dimensions.
   The DIMENSION statement is in the form

   DIMENSION $v_1(i_1)$, $v_2(i_2)$, ... $v_n(i_n)$

where each $v(i)$ is an array declarator.
   A COMMON statement is in the form

   COMMON $/x_1/a_1/$ ... $/(x_n/a_n)$

where each a is a nonempty list of variable names, array names, or array
declarators, and each x is a symbolic name or is empty. If x_1 is empty, the
first two slashes are optional. Each x is a block name, a name that bears no
relationship to any variable or array having the same name. This holds true
for any such variable or array in the same or any other program unit.
   With any given COMMON statement, entities occurring between block
name x and the next block name (or the end of the statement if no block
name follows) are declared to be in common block x. All entities from the
beginning of the statement until the appearance of a block name, or all entities in the statement if no block name appears, are declared to be in blank
or unlabeled common. Alternatively, the appearance of two slashes with no
block name between them declares the entities that follow to be in blank
common. The size of a common block in a program unit is the sum of the
storage required for the elements introduced through COMMON or EQUI-
VALENCE statements. Sizes of labeled common blocks with the same label
in the program units that comprise an executable program must be the
same. The sizes of blank common in the various program units that are to
be executed together need not be the same. Size is measured in terms of
storage units.

All program units of an executable program that contain any definition of a common block for a particular name define that block so that—

1. There is identity in type for all entities defined in the corresponding position from the beginning of that block.

2. If the block is labeled and the same number of entities is defined for the block, then the values in the corresponding positions (counted by the number of preceding storage units) are the same quantity in the executable program.

A double precision or a complex entity is counted as two logically consecutive storage units; a logical, real, or integer entity as one storage unit. Thus, the following is true for common blocks with the same number of storage units or for blank common:

1. In all program units that have defined the identical type to be given position (counted by the number of preceding storage units), references to that position refer to the same quantity.

2. A correct reference is made to a particular position, assuming a given type, if the most recent value assignment to that position was of the same type.

An EQUIVALENCE statement is in the form

EQUIVALENCE $(k_1), (k_2), \ldots, (k_n)$

where each k is a list in the form

$a_1, a_2, \ldots, a_m$

Each a is either a variable name or an array element name, the subscript of which contains only constants, and m is greater than or equal to 2. The number of subscript expressions of an array element name must be 1 or must correspond in number to the dimensionality of the array declarator.

The EQUIVALENCE statement is used to permit the sharing of storage by two or more entities. Each element in a given list is assigned to the same storage (or part of the same storage) by the processor. The EQUIVALENCE statement should not be used to equate two or more entities mathematically. If a two-storage-unit entity is made equivalent to a one-storage-unit entity, the latter will share space with the first storage unit of the former.

Assignment of storage to variables and arrays declared directly in a COMMON statement is determined solely by consideration of their type and the COMMON and array declarator statements. Entities so declared are always assigned unique storage, contiguous in the order declared in the COMMON statement.

When two variables or array elements share storage because of the effect of EQUIVALENCE statements, the symbolic names of the variables or arrays in question may not both appear in COMMON statements in the same program unit.

An EXTERNAL statement is in the form

EXTERNAL $v_1, v_2, \ldots, v_n$

where each v is an external procedure name. Appearance of a name in an EXTERNAL statement declares that name to be an external procedure name. If an external procedure name is used as an argument to another external procedure, it must appear in an EXTERNAL statement in the program unit in which it is so used.

A type statement is in the form

t $v_1, v_2, \ldots v_n$

where t is INTEGER, REAL, DOUBLE PRECISION, COMPLEX, or LOGICAL, and each v is a variable name, an array name, a function name, or an array declarator. A type statement is used to override or confirm the implicit typing, to declare entities as double precision, compex, or logical type, and it may supply dimension information. The appearance of a symbolic name in a type statement informs the processor that that variable is of the specified data type for all appearances in the program unit.

A data initialization statement is in the form:

DATA $k_1/d_1/,k_2/d_2/, \ldots k_n/d_n/$

where each k is a list containing names of variables and array elements and each d is a list of constants and optionally signed constants, any of which may be preceded by $j*$ (j is an integer constant). If a list contains more than one entry, the entries are separated by commas. Dummy arguments may not appear in the list k. Any subscript expression must be an integer constant. When the form $j*$ appears before a constant, it indicates that the constant is to be specified j times. A Hollerith constant may appear in the list d.

A data initialization statement is used to define initial values of variables or array elements. There must be a one-to-one correspondence between the list-specified item and the constants. By this correspondence, the initial value is established. An initially defined variable or array element may not be in blank common. A variable or array element in a labeled common block may be initially defined only in a block data subprogram.

The FORMAT statements are used in conjunction with the input/output of formatted records to provide conversion and editing information between the internal representation and the external character strings. A FORMAT statement is in the form

FORMAT $(q_1 t_1 z_1 t_2 z_2 \ldots t_n z_n q_2)$

where $(q_1 t_1 z_1 t_2 z_2 \ldots t_n z_n q_2)$ is the format specification, each q is a series of slashes or is empty, each t is a field descriptor or group of field descriptors, each z is a field separator, and n may be zero. Every FORMAT statement must be labeled.

The format field descriptors are of the forms srFw.d, srEw.d, srGw.d, srDw.d, rIw, rLw, rAw, $nHh_1 h_2 \ldots h_n$, nX, where the letters F, E, G, D, I, L, A, H, and X indicate the manner of conversion and editing between the internal and external representations and are called the conversion codes; w and n are nonzero integer constants representing the width of the field in the external character string; d is an integer constant representing the number of digits in the fractional part of the external character string (except for G conversion code); r, the repeat count, is an optional nonzero integer constant indicating the number of times to repeat the succeeding basic field descriptor; s is optional and represents a scale factor designator; and each h is one of the characters capable of representation by the processor. For all descriptors, the field width must be specified. For descriptors of the form w.d, the d must be specified even if it is zero. Further, w must be greater than or equal to d. The phrase "basic field descriptor" is used to signify the field descriptor unmodified by s or r. Internal representation of external fields corresponds to the internal representation of the corresponding type constants.

The format field separators are the slash and the comma. A series of slashes is also a field separator. The field descriptors or groups of field descriptors are separated by a field separator. A slash is used not only to separate field descriptors, but also to specify demarcation of formatted records. A formatted record is a string of characters. The lengths of the strings for a given external medium are dependent upon both the processor and the external medium. Processing of the number of characters that can be contained in a record by an external medium does not of itself cause the next record to be introduced or processed.

Repetition of the field descriptors (except nH and nX) is accomplished by using the repeat count. If the input/output list warrants, the specified conversion will be interpreted repetitively up to the specified number of times. A group of field descriptors or field separators can be repeated by enclosing them within parentheses and optionally preceding the left parenthesis with an integer constant called the "group repeat count," which indicates the number of times to interpret the enclosed grouping. If no group repeat count is specified, a group repeat count of 1 is assumed. This form of grouping is called a basic group. Further groupings may be formed by enclosing field descriptors, field separators, or basic groups within parentheses. Again, a group repeat count may be specified. The parentheses enclosing the format specification are not considered as group-delineating parentheses.

A scale factor designator is defined for use with the *F, E, G,* and *D* conversions and takes the form

    np

where *n,* the scale factor, is an integer constant or minus followed by an integer constant. When the format control is initiated, a scale factor of zero is established. Once a scale factor has been established, it applies to all subsequently interpreted *F, E, G,* and *D* field descriptors until another scale factor is encountered; then that scale factor is established.

The scale factor *n* affects the appropriate conversions in the following four ways:

1. For *F, E, G,* and *D* input conversions (provided no exponent exists in the external field), and *F* output conversions, the scale factor effect is that the externally represented number equals the internally represented number times the quantity 10 raised to the *n*th power.

2. The scale factor has no effect if there is an exponent in the external field.

3. For *E* and *D* output, the basic real constant part of the output quantity is multiplied by 10^n and the exponent is reduced by *n*.

4. For *G* output, the effect of the scale factor is suspended unless the magnitude of the data to be converted is outside the range that permits the effective use of *F* conversion. If the effective use of *E* conversion is required, the scale factor has the same effect as with *E* output.

The numeric field descriptors *I, F, E, G,* and *D* are used to specify input/output of integer, real, double precision, and complex data, as follows:

- With all numeric input conversions, leading blanks are not significant and other blanks are zero; plus signs may be omitted. A field of all blanks is considered zero.
- With the *F, E, G,* and *D* input conversions, a decimal point appearing in the input field overrides the decimal point specification supplied by the field descriptor.
- With all output conversions, the output field is right-justified. If the number of characters produced by the conversion is smaller than the field width, leading blanks will be inserted in the output field.

- With all output conversions, the external representation of a negative value must be signed; a positive value may be signed.
- The number of characters produced by an output conversion must not exceed the field width.

Appearance of the numeric field descriptor *Iw* indicates that the external field occupies *w* positions as an integer. The value of the list item appears, or is to appear, internally as integer data. In the external input field, the character string must be in the form of an integer constant or signed integer constant except for the interpretation of blanks. The external output field consists of blanks, if necessary followed by a minus when the value of the internal data is negative, or, otherwise, an optional plus followed by the magnitude of the internal value converted to an integer constant.

There are three conversions available for use with real data: *F, E,* and *G.* Appearance of the numeric field descriptor *Fw.d* indicates that the external field occupies *w* positions, the fractional part of which consists of *d* digits. The value of the list item appears, or is to appear, internally as real data. The basic form of the external input field consists of an optional sign preceding a string of digits optionally containing a decimal point. The basic form may be followed by an exponent of one of the following forms:

- Signed by integer constant.
- *E* followed by an integer constant.
- *E* followed by a signed integer constant.
- *D* followed by an integer constant.
- *D* followed by a signed integer constant.

An exponent containing *D* is equivalent to an exponent containing *E*. The external output field consists of blanks, if necessary, followed by a minus when the internal value is negative or an optional plus followed by a string of digits containing a decimal point representing the magnitude of the internal value, as modified by the established scale factor rounded to *d* fractional digits.

Appearance of the numeric field descriptor *Ew.d* indicates that the external field occupies *w* positions, the fractional part of which consists of *d* digits. The value of the list item appears, or is to appear, internally as real data. Form of the external input field is the same as for the *F* conversion.

Numeric field descriptor *Gw.d* indicates that the external field occupies *w* positions with *d* significant digits. The value of the list item appears, or is to appear, internally as real data. Input processing is the same as for the *F* conversion.

Numeric field descriptor $Dw.d$ indicates that the external field occupies w positions, the fractional part of which consists of d digits. The value of the list item appears, or is to appear, internally as double precision data. Basic form of the external input field is the same as for real conversions. The external output field is the same as for the E conversion, except that the character D may replace the character E in the exponent.

Since complex data consists of a pair of separate real data, the conversion is specified by two successively interpreted real field descriptors. The first of these supplies the real part; the second supplies the imaginary part.

Appearance of the logical field descriptor Lw indicates that the external field occupies w positions as a string of information, as defined in subsequent paragraphs. The list item appears, or is to appear, internally as logical data. The external input field must consist of optional blanks followed by a T or F and by optional characters for TRUE and FALSE. The external output field consists of $w-1$ blanks followed by a T or F as the value of the internal data is TRUE or FALSE.

Hollerith information may be transmitted by means of two field descriptors, nH and Aw: nH causes Hollerith information to be read into or written from the n characters (including blanks) following the nH descriptor in the format; Aw causes w Hollerith characters to be read into or written from a specified list.

The field descriptor for blanks is nX. On input, n characters of the external input record are skipped. On output, n blanks are inserted in the external output record.

Any of the formatted input/output statements may contain an array name in place of the reference to a FORMAT statement label. At the time an array is referenced in such a manner, the first part of the information contained in the array, taken in the natural order, must constitute a valid format specification. There is no requirement on the information contained in the array following the right parenthesis that ends the format specification. The format specification to be inserted in the array has the same form as that defined for a FORMAT statement; that is, it begins with a left parenthesis and ends with a right parenthesis. An nH field descriptor may not be part of a format specification within an array. This format specification may be inserted in the array by use of a data initialization statement, or by use of a READ statement together with an A format.

Function and subprogram defining statements are discussed in the next section.

Procedures and Subprograms

Four categories of procedures are available in FORTRAN: statement functions, intrinsic functions, external functions, and external subroutines. The first three categories are referred to collectively as functions, or function procedures; the last, as subroutines or subroutine procedures. Also available are two categories of subprograms: procedure subprograms and specification subprograms. Function subprograms and subroutine subprograms are classified as procedure subprograms. Block data subprograms are classified as specification subprograms.

A statement function is defined internally in the program unit in which it is referenced. Definition is a single statement similar in form to an arithmetic or logical assignment statement. In a given program unit, all statement function definitions must precede the first executable statement of the program unit and must follow the specification statements, if any. The name of a statement function must not appear in an EXTERNAL statement or as a variable name or an array name in the same program unit. A statement function is defined by a statement in the form

$$f(a_1, a_2, \ldots, a_n) = e$$

where f is the function name and e is an expression. The a are distinct variable names, called the dummy arguments of the function. Since these are dummy arguments, their names, which serve only to indicate type, number, and order of arguments, may be the same as variable names of the same type appearing elsewhere in the program unit. Aside from the dummy arguments, the expression e may only contain non-Hollerith constants, variable references, intrinsic function references, references to previously defined statement functions, and external function references.

A statement function is referenced by using its reference as a primary in an arithmetic or logic expression. The actual arguments, which constitute the argument list, must agree in order, number, and type with the corresponding dummy arguments. An actual argument in a statement function reference may be any expression of the same type as the corresponding dummy argument. Execution of a statement function reference results in an association of actual arguments in the expression of the function definition, and an evaluation of the expression. Following this, the resultant value is made available to the expression that contained the function reference.

The symbolic names of the intrinsic functions (see Table E-6) are predefined to the processor. An intrinsic function is referenced by using its reference as a primary in an arithmetic or logical expression. The actual arguments, which constitute the argument list, must agree in type, number, and order with the specification in Table E-6 and may be any expression of the specified type. Intrinsic functions AMOD, MOD, SIGN, ISIGN, and DSIGN are not defined when the value of the second argument is zero.

An external function is defined externally to the program unit that references it. When it is defined by FORTRAN statements headed by a FUNCTION statement, it is called a function subprogram. A FUNCTION statement takes the form

$$t \text{ FUNCTION } f(a_1, a_2 \ldots, a_n)$$

where t is either INTEGER, REAL, DOUBLE PRECISION, COMPLEX, or LOGICAL, or is empty; f is the symbolic name of the function to be defined; and the a, called the dummy arguments, are each either a variable name, an array name, or an external procedure name. Function subprograms are constructed with the following restrictions:

1. The symbolic name of the function must also appear as a variable name in the defining subprogram. During every execution of the subprogram, this variable must be defined and, once defined, may be referenced or redefined. The value of the variable at the time of execution of any RETURN statement in this subprogram is called the "value" of the function.

2. The symbolic name of the function must not appear in any nonexecutable statement in this program unit, except as the symbolic name of the function in the FUNCTION statement.

3. The symbolic names of the dummy arguments may not appear in an EQUIVALENCE, COMMON, or DATA statement in the function subprogram.

4. The function subprogram may define or redefine one or more of its arguments so as to return results in addition to the value of the function.

5. The function subprogram may contain any statements except BLOCK DATA, SUBROUTINE, another FUNCTION statement, or any statement that directly or indirectly references the function being defined.

6. The function subprogram must contain at least one RETURN statement.

An external function is located by using its reference as a primary in an arithmetic or logical expression. The actual arguments, which constitute the program list, must agree in order, number, and type with the corresponding dummy arguments in the defining program unit. An actual argument in an external function reference may be one of the following:

- A variable name.
- An array element name.
- An array name.
- Any other expression.
- The name of an external procedure.

Table E-6. ANSI Internal Functions (Cont'd.)

FUNCTION	NUMBER OF ARGUMENTS	SYMBOLIC NAME	TYPE OF ARGUMENT	TYPE OF FUNCTION
Basic External Functions				
Exponential	1	EXP	Real	Real
	1	DEXP	Double	Double
	1	CEXP	Complex	Complex
Natural logarithm	1	ALOG	Real	Real
	1	DLOG	Double	Double
	1	CLOG	Complex	Complex
Common logarithm	1	ALOGIO	Real	Real
		DLOGIO	Double	Double
Trigonometric sine	1	SIN	Real	Real
	1	DSIN	Double	Double
	1	CSIN	Complex	Complex
Trigonometric cosine	1	COS	Real	Real
	1	DCOS	Double	Double
	1	CCOS	Complex	Complex
Hyperbolic tangent	1	TANH	Real	Real
Square root	1	SQRT	Real	Real
	1	DSQRT	Double	Double
	1	CSQRT	Complex	Complex
Arctangent	1	ATAN	Real	Real
	1	DATAN	Double	Double
	2	ATAN2	Real	Real
	2	DATAN2	Double	Double
Remaindering	2	DMOD	Double	Double
Modulus	1	CABS	Complex	Real

The FORTRAN processors must supply the external functions listed in Table E-6. Arguments for which the result of these functions is not mathematically defined, or of a type other than that specified, are improper.

An external subroutine is defined externally to the program unit that references it. When defined by FORTRAN statements headed by a SUBROUTINE statement, it is called a subroutine subprogram. A SUBROUTINE statement is of one of the forms

SUBROUTINE s $(a_1, a_2, \ldots, a_n)$
SUBROUTINE s

where *s* is the symbolic name of the subroutine to be defined and the *a*s, called the dummy arguments, are each either a variable name, an array name, or an external procedure name. Subroutine subprograms are constructed with the following restrictions:

1. The symbolic name of the subroutine must not appear in any statement in this subprogram except as the symbolic name of the subroutine in the SUBROUTINE statement itself.

2. The symbolic names of the dummy arguments may not appear in an EQUIVALENCE, COMMON, or DATA statement in the subprogram.

3. The subroutine subprogram may define or redefine one or more of its arguments so as to return results.

4. The subroutine subprogram may contain any statements except BLOCK DATA, FUNCTION, another SUBROUTINE statement, or any statement that directly or indirectly references the subroutine being defined.

5. The subroutine subprogram must contain at least one RETURN statement.

A subroutine is referenced by a CALL statement. The actual arguments, which constitute the argument list, must agree in order, number, and type with the corresponding dummy arguments in the defining program. Use of a Hollerith constant as an actual argument is an exception to the rule requiring agreement of type. An actual argument in a subroutine reference may be one of the following:

- A Hollerith constant.
- A variable name.
- An array element name.
- An array name.
- Any other expression.
- The name of an external procedure.

If an actual argument is an external function name or a subroutine name, the corresponding dummy argument must be used as an external function name or a subroutine name.

A BLOCK DATA statement takes the form

BLOCK DATA

This statement may appear only as the first statement of specification subprograms that are called block data subprograms, and which are used to enter initial values into elements of labeled common blocks. This special subprogram contains only type statements, EQUIVALENCE, DATA, DIMENSION, and COMMON statements.

If any entity of a given common block is being given an initial value in such a subprogram, a complete set of specification statements for the entire block must be included, even though some of the elements of the block do not appear in DATA statements. Initial values may be entered into more than one block in a single subprogram.

Programs

An executable program is a collection of statements, comment lines, and end lines that completely (except for input data values and their effects) describe a computing procedure.

In a program part there must be at least one executable statement and there may be FORMAT statements and data initialization statements. It need not contain any statement from either of the latter two classes. This collection of statements may optionally be preceded by statement function definitions, data initialization statements, and FORMAT statements. As before, none or only some of these need be present.

A program body consists of a program part followed by an end line. These can be preceded by specification statements and/or FORMAT statement.

Composition of a subprogram includes a SUBROUTINE or FUNCTION statement followed by a program body; otherwise, it is a block data subprogram.

A block data subprogram is a BLOCK DATA statement, followed by the appropriate specification statements, followed by data initialization statements, and then an end line.

A main program consists of a program body. An executable program consists of a main program plus any number of subprograms, external procedures, or both. A program unit is a main program or a subprogram.

When an executable program begins operation, execution commences with the start of the first executable statement of the main program. A subprogram, when referenced, starts execution with the beginning of the first executable statement of that subprogram. Unless a statement is a GO TO, arithmetic IF, RETURN, or STOP statement or the terminal statement of a DO, completion of execution of that statement causes execution of the next following executable statement. A program part may not contain an executable statement that can never be executed. Each program part must contain a first executable statement.

FEATURES OF ANSI BASIC FORTRAN

This section discusses those features of ANSI Basic FORTRAN that differ from those of ANSI FORTRAN.

Program Form   The currency symbol $ is excluded from the ANSI Basic FORTRAN character set. Only 5 continuation lines are permitted, in contrast to 19 lines in ANSI FORTRAN. Also, the maximum size of a statement label is reduced from five to four digits and symbolic names may be up to five characters, in contrast to six characters in ANSI FORTRAN.

Data Types   Double precision, complex, logical, and Hollerith data types are not available in ANSI Basic FORTRAN.

Data and Procedure Identification   Double precision, complex, logical, and Hollerith constants are not available in ANSI Basic FORTRAN.

Expressions   Neither relational nor logical expressions are permitted in Basic FORTRAN.

Statements   The following statement features are not available in ANSI Basic FORTRAN:

- Logical and GO TO assignment statements are not available.
- Neither assigned GO TO nor logical IF statements are available.
- A maximum of four octal digits are permitted, compared to five in ANSI FORTRAN.
- The extended range of DO loop is not allowed.
- No print carriage control is provided for formatted output records.
- No array declaration is permitted in a COMMON statement.
- No three-dimensional arrays or subscripts are allowed.
- Adjustable dimension is not possible.
- Labeled common blocks are not permitted.
- The EXTERNAL statement is not allowed.
- Type statements (INTEGER, REAL, DOUBLE PRECISION, COMPLEX, or LOGICAL) are not available.
- A data initialization statement is not available.
- The scale factor is not provided.
- A, G, D, complex, and logical data conversions are not available.
- Formats may not be specified in arrays.
- The intrinsic function set does not include truncation, remaindering, maximums, or minimums.
- Double precision and complex functions are not included.
- External functions may not alter variables in common or variables associated with common via an EQUIVALENCE statement.
- The basic external function set does not include common logarithm or any double precision or complex functions.
- The BLOCK DATA subprograms are not permitted.

Table E-6. ANSI Internal Functions

FUNCTION	NUMBER OF ARGUMENTS	SYMBOLIC NAME	TYPE OF ARGUMENT	TYPE OF FUNCTION
Intrinsic Functions				
Absolute value	1	ABS	Real	Real
		IABS	Integer	Integer
		DABS	Double	Double
Truncation	1	AINT	Real	Real
		INT	Real	Integer
		IDINT	Double	Integer
Remaindering	2	AMOD	Real	Real
		MOD	Integer	Integer
Choosing largest value	≥2	AMAXO	Integer	Real
		AMAXI	Real	Real
		MAXO	Integer	Integer
		MAXI	Real	Integer
		DMAXI	Double	Double
Choosing smallest value	≥2	AMINO	Integer	Real
		AMINI	Real	Real
		MINO	Integer	Integer
		MINI	Real	Integer
		DMINI	Double	Double
Float	1	FLOAT	Integer	Real
Fix	1	IFIX	Real	Integer
Transfer of sign	2	SIGN	Real	Real
		ISIGN	Integer	Integer
		DSIGN	Double	Double
Positive difference	2	DIM	Real	Real
		IDIM	Integer	Integer
Obtain most significant part of double precision argument	1	SNGL	Double	Real
Obtain real part of complex argument	1	REAL	Complex	Real
Obtain imaginary part of complex argument	1	AIMAG	Complex	Real
Express single precision argument in double precision form	1	DBLE	Real	Double
Express two real arguments in complex form	2	CMPLX	Real	Complex
Obtain conjugate of a complex argument	1	CONJG	Complex	Complex

APPENDIX F:
MINICOMPUTER APPLICATION AREAS

CHARACTERISTICS	APPLICATION AREA				
	INDUSTRIAL CONTROL	PERIPHERAL CONTROL	COMMUNICATIONS	COMPUTATION	DATA ACQUISITION
Use	Industrial testing (of components, systems, etc.), numerical control of machine tools, typesetting, control of open- or closed-loop continuous processes.	Controls operation of other equipment, such as terminals, subsystems connected to larger computers, or data entry systems.	Line concentrator to reduce number of transmission lines required for data transfer; information flow controller at a node in a message switching system network; front-end communication controller for large computer system.	Traditional computer jobs—business processing, scientific computation, software development; either stand-alone configuration or time-sharing system.	Controls collection of data, frequently at high rates and large quantities, for subsequent processing elsewhere; monitors instrumentation.
Where Found	Throughout all types of industry-electronic component fabrication, chemical process control, navigation systems, aircraft checkout systems.	Associated with larger computer systems as a controller of local or remote peripheral devices.	High-volume communication networks, e.g., airline reservation systems, stock quotation systems; internal message systems in large companies;	In all types of businesses, especially in smaller firms, colleges, high schools; also in larger firms needing decentralized computing or in-house time sharing, e.g., manufacturers utilities, engineering, R&D, and consulting organizations.	Industry and military, e.g., experimental systems, R&D organizations, satellite telemetering systems, laboratories, hospitals.
Application Requirements and Needs	Operation to be controlled or tested must be realistically definable by a mathematical analog; high reliability; must be capable of operating in a hostile environment; system design must have process orientation.	Efficient interface, high data rates, ability to handle wide range of signal requirements; software compatibility; special need to establish, and operate under, worse-case conditions: system design must have task orientation.	Large transaction volume to justify savings in line charges; adequate buffering to withstand wide range of message load while not losing transactions.	High computation speeds in time-sharing and scientific applications; variety of peripheral devices to satisfy a variety of input/output needs in business applications; extensive system and application software support.	High data transfer rates, high-speed/high-capacity peripheral storage; editing and formatting tasks, but usually only simple processing/logical task.
Market Segment— OEM or End User	Both OEM and end user.	Principally OEM.	Both OEM and end user.	Both OEM and end user.	Principally end user.
Customer Characteristics	Usually highly technical but frequently not experienced in computer systems.	Usually highly technical and with extensive experience in computer systems usage and design; highly price sensitive.	OEM's technically oriented, end users application—and software-oriented.	Often only modest computer systems experience, but strong application knowledge; often a narrow perspective of potential system use; quite price conscious.	Mostly technical with extensive systems capability; emphasis on performance more than economics.
Minicomputer's Functions	Accepts process condition signals directly from process instrumentation, applies these signals to prestored mathematical analog to determine process parameter correction signals to operator or directly to process.	Processes interrupt requests, or initiates action itself; outputs control signals to one or more peripheral devices which respond by taking the desired action; frequently involved with sequencing, data transfer, buffering, editing, and formatting.	As a line concentrator, receives data on several low-speed lines, interleaves characters, and transmits data on one high-speed line; in message switching, accepts messages from multiple sources & coordinates their output on multiple output lines, logs transactions, and verifies transmission; as communications front end, processor performs on-line monitoring, data editing, and formatting.	Takes input from a variety of peripheral devices, processes data with prestored programs or compiles/assembles new programs being developed; outputs results to user via printer, display, etc.; in time sharing, handles multiple jobs concurrently without unacceptable degradation of service to any user.	Accepts input from one or multiple sources usually at high and variable rates; edits, formats, stores raw data, preprocesses data for later processing; logs selected data.